CAPITALISM CAN SURVIVE
IN A
NO-GROWTH ECONOMY

Also by Herbert N. Woodward

THE HUMAN DILEMMA

ČAPITALISM CAN SURVIVE IN A NO-GROWTH ECONOMY

HERBERT N. WOODWARD

THE BROOKDALE PRESS
In association with
WALKER AND COMPANY

PERMISSIONS

The author has received from the *Harvard Business Review* permission to use material from his article in the Jan. Feb., 1976 issue of that magazine.

Permission has also been received for reprinting material from his article in *Business and Society Review*, Winter 1975, Volume 16, Copyright 1976, Warren, Gorham and Lamont, Inc., 210 South Street, Boston, Mass. All Rights Reserved.

In addition, the following permissions have been received to reprint excerpts from material written by others:

"The Tragedy of the Commons," Garrett Hardin, *Science*, Vol. 162, pp. 1243–1248, Dec. 13, 1968. Copyright 1968 by the American Association for Advancement of Science.

"Ethics and the Corporation," Irving Kristol, *The Wall Street Journal,* April 16, 1975.

The American Condition, Copyright © 1974 by Richard N. Goodwin. Reprinted by permission of Doubleday & Company, Inc.

Library of Congress Cataloging in Publication Data
Woodward, Herbert Norton
Capitalism can survive in a no-growth economy.
Bibliography: p.
Includes index.
1.   Economic development.
2.   Capitalism.
3.   Big business.
4.   Work.   I.   Title.   II.   Title:
No-growth economy:
HC59.W6155   330.12'2   76-12887
ISBN 0-8027-0554-5 (Walker)

For information, address the publisher:
THE BROOKDALE PRESS
184 *Brookdale Road,*
Stamford, Connecticut 06903

ISBN: 0-8027-0554-5
Library of Congress Catalog Number: 76-12887

Manufactured in the United States of America by
RAY FREIMAN & COMPANY

For Nancy

ACKNOWLEDGMENTS

Some may write books easily, tossing off page after page with skill and flourish. I do not. One rough draft follows another with liberal use of scissors and stapler to reorganize the ideas which are painfully difficult to put into shape.

Obsession with my own words and phrases often blinds me to misuse of words, clichés, and inconsistencies. Fortunately, I have been blessed with friends who have read critically my early attempts at coherence. Warren A. Johnson read the second draft and helped to redirect my approach. Edward G. Broenniman and Louis Cheskin plowed through the next draft and added their valuable analyses. My friend Waldo W. Ranson provided helpful advice and counsel. Ray Freiman, my publisher, guided me through the editing and publishing maze at all stages, using his vast skill, experience and knowledge. Ireta Jimmie has typed each draft speedily and well, making early publication possible. I am grateful to them all. The contents of this book, of course, are entirely my own responsibility.

Every time I work through the text, I find weaknesses that demand attention. I am like the engineer who is never satisfied with the product he has designed. The manager in me finally insists that I stop designing and go into production. Which I have done.

HNW

Contents

"A man's a fool to use the prophet's trade.
For if he happens to bring bitter news
He's hated by the men for whom he works;
And if he pities them and tells them lies
He wrongs the gods. No prophet but Apollo
Should sing to men, for he has nought to fear."
Teiresias in Euripides,
THE PHOENICIAN WOMEN,
lines 954–959

Translator: Elizabeth Wykoff

1

It's a Small World

EVER SINCE THE INDUSTRIAL REVOLUTION BEGAN, we have associated success with growth. The capitalistic free enterprise system, we are told, depends on continuing growth for its vitality.

But growth cannot continue forever. In the very last few years, we can sense more and more that we are reaching the end of an era, because the limitations of our world are pressing closer on us. The public has just begun to be aware of some basic long-range world problems.

In this book I am not trying to provide the proof that a steady-state (no-growth) world is not far ahead, although I will review some of the argument. Many qualified writers have made this point abundantly clear (see my bibliography for some of the best). There is little disagreement that population growth, in particular, cannot go on forever; the differences in opinion are about how urgent the problem is.

We all bring our own emotional biases to the analysis of basic economic issues. If we would happily see the Establishment confounded and overturned, we are more willing to accept predictions of disaster. Contrariwise, if our future and our family's future depends on maintenance of the status quo, we tend to give doomsayers short shrift.

If there is such a thing as the Establishment, I am a part of it. I am a capitalist born and bred and believe in capitalism's strength and its benefits to everyone. But the built-in bias can be identified and compensated for. I recognize that we had all better open our minds. I find myself objective enough to recognize that we must think seriously about our human future, for we do indeed have problems, and they will not go away.

Our basic long-range world problems may be summed up in three words: population, energy, environment. Individually, each of these three groups of problems has concerned many people for years, but their convergence into different aspects of a single world problem is new.

Population, energy, and environment are intimately interrelated. Let me illustrate. In earlier days, when population was small and resource—and energy—use was moderate, pollution was not a problem. Earlier in this century, for example, the cities and towns bordering the Mississippi could dump their sewage into it raw and untreated, yet the river's ecosystem could absorb and cleanse it so that most of the river stayed relatively pure. Such pollution is a serious problem today primarily because a denser population produces a vast tonnage of sewage which overpowers the ecosystem.

Look at another aspect of the single problem: if fossil fuels were unlimited in supply, we would have enough cheap energy available to do all the work necessary to clean our environment, even if world population continued to grow. But fossil fuel energy is finite in quantity and is becoming more expensive to find and extract. Only if and when we learn to obtain power economically by nuclear fusion will we have virtually infinite energy available to us. Today, no one knows whether that can ever be possible. Increase of population will increase pollution even faster, but energy won't be available to keep it under control.

The environment itself would be no problem if our planet were far larger in size and we had extensive new areas to develop. In that case, we could spread out our population into the new lands, and the larger ecosystem could absorb all our activities without trouble, even if we had a much bigger population and caused even more pollution by the use of more fuel energy per capita than we do now.

It is the combination of high (and growing) world population, high (and increasing) use of fuel energy per capita, the finite size of our planet and the limited absorptive capability of its ecological system that is doing us in. Solve completely any one of the three aspects of the total problem and we have a new lease on planetary human life. Since rapidly increasing world population is crammed into the same limited space, while using an increasing amount of energy, something has to give. Inevitably our environment will deteriorate further unless we can spare ever more energy to cope with it.

In the not-too-long run, so long as there is no additional space, and assuming that energy supply is ultimately limited, there are only two possible courses of action (or a combination of them):

1   Reduce per-capita use of energy faster than population increases.

2 Stop population growth (and eventually reduce world population to a lower and healthier figure).

Between now and the end of the century, no one expects that population growth can even be stopped, let alone reversed, by any known method short of increasing the death rate. In the short run, therefore, we may have no choice except a sharp reduction in per capita energy consumption.

Different aspects of the total problem have been discussed in a variety of publications, a few of which have appeared on the public newsstands (for instance, Rachel Carson's *Silent Spring,* Harrison Brown's *The Challenge of Man's Future,* Barry Commoner's *The Closing Circle,* and Paul Ehrlich's *The Population Bomb*).

The real explosion of awareness came, however, when the Club of Rome, an informal international organization concerned with man's future, sponsored the publication of *The Limits to Growth* in 1972[1]. In this book, an MIT group comprising experts in a variety of disciplines published their analysis of a computer study purporting to show what would happen to the human economy in the next century and a quarter. No matter what adjustments were made in the program, the computer study showed that early in the next century the world economy must end in a collapse in which hunger, disease, and social disruption would drastically cut our human population.

The Limits to Growth had a major impact. The results were unexpectedly shocking. It stimulated wild dissent from all directions. It was attacked for its superficiality, its methodology and its substance. It was subjected to a bombardment such as few books have ever survived. After several years, however, it

4

may be said that it has come through this onslaught, scarred but not basically hurt.

A follow-up report by a different group at the Club of Rome, *Mankind at the Turning Point*,[2] has built upon its predecessors' work and profited from their critics by analyzing the world situation more thoroughly by different regions. Its conclusions modify only slightly the gloomy forecast of *The Limits to Growth*.

Population growth is the most serious of the three problems, largely because its momentum is so difficult to stop and takes so long to change.

Assuming that the world (and the United States) must eventually stop growing in population and in energy use per capita, how will this come about? And when? The so-called experts find no agreement in answering either of these questions. The world population passed the four billion mark in 1975. In 1650 it was only half a billion. It doubled to one billion by 1825 (175 years later), doubled again to two billion by 1930 (105 more years) and has doubled again in the remaining forty-five years. At the accelerating rate of increase, it could double again to eight billion soon after the year 2000, only twenty-four years away.

U.S. population is still increasing, although not at so rapid a pace. Late in 1972, the U.S. birth rate dropped below the replacement rate of 2.11 births for each woman during her child-bearing years. But that does not mean that U.S. population has leveled out, as many people believe.

The figures are correct, but the assumption is false. The Bureau of the Census Population Estimates and Projections of October, 1975, show that if fertility remains at 2.1 per woman hereafter, the present population of about 213,000,000 will rise to 294,000,000 in the year 2020 (only forty-four years away) and will still be climbing, although slowly. Even if the rate drops to 1.7 births per woman, the population will rise to 252,000,000 by 2020 A.D.

How can this be? Increase in population is the net excess of births over deaths. Population climbs when more people are born than die in a given period. The present average age of the American population is only 28, but the average length of life is 69, so that, as a percentage of total population, the number of deaths are quite low, now and in the near future, because old people are a relatively small fraction of our present population. Or, to look at the other side of the same picture, the great majority of our female population is either still in the child-bearing years or will enter them during the next sixteen years. If each woman has an average of 2.11 children, the population will continue to climb until it levels out about seventy years from now. The extra 0.11 child allows for children who do not live to child-bearing age and for the birth of slightly more male than female children. Seventy years from now, the average age of the population will have increased substantially and the pattern of age distribution will be similar to that of Sweden today, with a somewhat higher average age than we now have.

Although the present birth rate is below 2.11 children per female during her lifetime, history gives us no assurance that it will stay that low. In the past, whenever the birth rate has declined sharply, there has been a tendency to be concerned about underpopulation, so that the curve tended to turn upward again. This may well happen again.

The Bureau of Census in 1975 made one more fertility assumption. If the birth rate becomes 2.7 per woman, the population in 2020 will reach 362,000,000. If the birth rate remains that high, the population will still be climbing rapidly, unless the death rate turns upward.

U.S. population seems to be gradually leveling out, however, as it is in most of the industrialized world. (East Germany, West Germany and Luxembourg have actually stopped growing in population.) In the underdeveloped world, although birth rates are gradually declining, the net increase in population is close to 3% per year. A 3% annual increase for 100 years results in a nineteenfold increase. (In other words, a population of 1,000,000 growing at 3% per year compounded, becomes 19,000,000 at the end of a century.) If this figure seems impossibly high to you, take out your calculator and check it yourself. You will understand better what exponential growth means.

Turn from population to energy. While population is not increasing rapidly in the developed world, per capita use of energy is, particularly since World War II. In the United States, a few comparative percentage increases from 1946 to 1968 have been:

Population	43%
Motor Fuel Comsumption	100%
Electric Power	276%
Synthetic Organic Chemicals	495%
Plastics	1,024%[3]

(Of course, particularly in the case of the last two examples cited, the starting base was low.) We have all heard that the United States, with 5.4% of the world's population, is now using over 30% of its resources. The leveling off of U.S. population does not entitle us to be complacent. Considering the total population–energy–environment relationship, we are in deep trouble.

Population growth will not come to a sudden halt because of any sharp voluntary decline in the birth rate. Even if the world were to achieve a replacement birth rate instantaneously, world population would continue to grow for another seventy years, until the average age increased enough so that births and deaths were equal. But even if world population could become zero-growth right now (which could be achieved only by an immediate drastic decrease in the birth rate or a major increase in the death rate, or both), the need for food (and, therefore, energy) would continue to mount because of the subsequent increase in average age of its population. In the underdeveloped world, the average age is around 15; as the young become mature they have to eat more to live. "If ZPG became a reality in India today, 25–30 percent more food would still be needed within a decade."[4]

Increasing population numbers, increasing cost and decreasing availability of energy, combined with environmental pollution, are closing in on us. We are in deep trouble, although we are still hardly aware of our problem. Since we are not willing to move to protect our future by both halting population growth and reducing energy consumption, the trends we have set in motion will continue. Therefore, something will have to give, and relatively soon.

We had our first preliminary signs in 1973. The Arab oil embargo gave us a mild preview of what an energy-scarce society would have to face. In 1974, the famines in the African Sahel and food shortages elsewhere in the underdeveloped world gave notice that there is little or no surplus world food

8

supply. We have quickly forgotten both scares, but the situation has been alleviated only temporarily.

If an American argues that is is appropriate to have more children because he can personally afford them, remember that each American child uses more energy and resources in its first six months of life than the average native of India uses in a lifetime. We are incredible energy hogs, and are doing far more than our share in dooming our descendants to grinding poverty and inevitable early death.

Food is our most vulnerable resource. Human population is increasing at the rate of about 76 million a year. Food supplies have barely kept abreast of this increase, to a considerable extent because of an accelerated use of energy in the form of farm machinery and nitrogen fertilizer to intensify per-acre yields. The law of diminishing returns is taking effect, and the margin of safety is getting rapidly smaller. One bad world harvest now can doom tens of millions of people to famine and death.

I do not like being a doomsayer. In predicting widespread tragedy, however, I am only echoing the thoughts of a host of humane and dedicated scientists, engineers, ecologists, and philosophers. Notably absent from the voices of concern are those of the great mass of economists. In general, economists wear blinders and look only at the figures of their own arcane discipline. They have assumed that ecology is a branch of economics, instead of the other way around. Therefore, with a few notable exceptions, they have not looked at our ecological system at all.

Population can and eventually must be brought within limits. When we turn to energy, however, our problem is that there is too little, not too much, of it. We rely heavily on the fossil fuels (oil, natural gas and coal) which were laid down during the dinosaur ages millions of years ago. These fuels, which took an incredible period of time to form, have been used up at an accelerating rate in little more than a century. They will not last forever.

While fifty years ago the United States relied primarily on coal, our present economy is based largely on the use of oil and natural gas, which have been cheap, clean, efficient, and available in vast quantity. The recent manifold increase in the price of Middle Eastern oil, upon which we are increasingly dependent, has had a dramatic effect, however, in discouraging use of oil and encouraging a kind of enforced conservation. We have not yet felt the full impact of these price increases. But the law of supply and demand is already functioning: as the price has risen, consumption has leveled off and even declined a little.

The world's oil is far from exhausted, although the supply is ultimately finite. In the last analysis, it is a matter of price, which takes into account both supply and demand. To the extent that we can wean ourselves from utter dependence on this beautiful fluid, the demand will decrease. Our first convulsive reaction to the new high prices eased demand to the point that the Organization of Petroleum Exporting Countries (OPEC) considered price reductions, but not for long. The prices have gone up again. On the supply side, higher wellhead prices undoubtedly encourage exploration and drilling for new finds in the United States. We must, however, be aware that it does not pay to expend more energy to get it out than is extracted. If there is no net energy gain by that rule, it is not worth drilling for at any price.

We know that domestic production of oil peaked in the United States in 1970 (the date predicted years before by

M. King Hubbert of the U.S. Geological Survey) and that the oil from the Alaska North Slope, which we expect will start flowing in 1977, will scarcely replace the decline in production from the other forty-nine states. Therefore, unless our per capita use of oil is gradually reduced, our dependence on foreign oil can only increase.

Since we have so many people and use so much oil, we have to get our supplies wherever we can, and pay top price. Admittedly, our per-capita consumption of oil is excessively high. We can probably cut it at least a third by proper conservation practices. But that would only be a reprieve, because our domestic production and supplies will continue to decline and our population will keep on climbing. The Arabs, to the extent that they can agree among themselves, will have the power, and every incentive, to charge as much as the traffic will bear.

In the not-too-long run, we must find and use other kinds of energy. The doomsayers have been ridiculed because they do not believe that technology will always come up with an answer to our energy problem. After all, when wood began to run out as a fuel, coal was discovered and used. And then came oil. Something is bound to turn up, the optimists say.

Perhaps. But ought we not hedge our bets? Prospects for eventual relief may be good—but when?

Earlier prospects of mammoth supplies of substitute energy from oil shale now have faded because of evaluation of the high cost and tremendous environmental problems involved in its extraction. Hopes for development of the Athabaska tar sands in Canada have dimmed for similar reasons. The net energy calculations of Howard T. Odum (Graduate Professor of Environmental Engineering at the University of Florida) show that recovery from these sources will require more input of energy than can be gotten out, regardless of price (UPI dispatch, March 9, 1975).

Hopes for vast energy from nuclear fission plants have also declined. Nuclear energy is still an insignificant power source in the United States; it has just passed firewood as an energy source. Present nuclear fission methods depend on supplies of uranium which may not be sufficient for the kind of increase in production that would be called for if a significant addition is to be made to our power supply. In net energy terms, nuclear energy yields only two to three calories for each calorie put in. Safety is a major unsolved problem, not just for waste disposal, but also for plant operation itself.

Development of the liquid metal breeder reactor, which would solve any problem of uranium shortage, has been slow. Now we are pondering whether we are willing to make the Faustian bargain to obtain its power at the risk (bordering on certainty) that nuclear accidents will devastate us or that the waste products which lose only half their strength in 24,000 years will poison us or future generations (plutonium being the most toxic substance known).

Among the fossil fuels, coal has the most promise. Enough coal is available to supply us for hundreds of years, although the cost of extraction and the environmental problems involved in obtaining it are serious handicaps to any easy solution. Odum calculates that stripmined western coal will produce three calories for every calorie required to produce it. (This compares to a 6½:1 energy ratio for Arab oil.)

Nuclear fusion, duplicating the process which heats the sun, is the best long-range hope for limitless power. Although a few laboratory breakthroughs have been made, it is too soon to tell if this source of power will ever be commercially available. In any event, it is at least a quarter century away.

We are beginning to look at solar energy as our ultimate answer. It is inexhaustible, tremendous in amount, relatively constant in availability and non-polluting. A generation ago, considerable progress was made in practical development of one important aspect of solar power: wind energy. Thousands of farms relied on windmills for water pumping, power generation and other work. But in the thirties, the Rural Electrification Administration ran power lines to the most remote farms providing cheap electric power, thus making windmills unnecessary. We had better start using windpower again and all other possible means of harnessing the power of the sun. We are just beginning to explore the possibilities. The capital investment necessary to make solar energy widely available will be immense, but so are the capital requirements of all the alternatives being considered.

If there is no easy or early solution to our energy problem, we are going to be forced to conserve its use. The increasing cost of oil (and natural gas) will be the major stimulus to conservation. The full effects of these higher costs will be felt over the next few years.

Advocates of continued growth argue that the price mechanism will automatically solve all scarcity problems, in that, as supply of any resource diminishes, demand will be controlled by the rise in price that the scarcity causes. If, for instance, the price of tin were to quintuple because of unavailability, the argument is that two things would happen: 1) the higher price would encourage greater development of marginal methods of tin extraction, thus helping the supply situation, and

2) it would encourage substitution of other materials for tin. These arguments are only partly true. Higher prices will eventually discourage some of the uses of tin, but, for some applications, no other material may do the job at all. Higher prices will, to some extent, both stimulate supply and reduce demand.

The price mechanism alleviates supply problems of minerals only when there are abundant lower grade ores available which become economical to mine as the price increases, or if there really are substitute materials available at higher prices. But what if the ores are not available at all except in high grade lodes? Or there is no good substitute at all? Higher prices cannot stimulate the extraction of additional supply if there is none left.

The value of potential future resources is discounted by our market structure so that they are given little weight in determining current prices. Price forces are so shortsighted that we are likely to run wide open in our use of tin until it is too late to conserve supplies for essential needs for future years.

To date, however, threats of imminent exhaustion of reserves of particular minerals have proved premature. So far, despite steadily increasing use, nothing has run out, although we have to go farther from home, dig deeper, and settle for lower grade ores.

New reserves have been uncovered as fast as old ones are exhausted. Thus, the argument that high prices will solve scarcity problems has some merit, particularly when applied to mineral resources. When prices go up, we use less; call it conservation. Next, we may find substitutes for the scarce material. Finally, provided sufficient energy is available, we can dig still deeper to recover the less-accessible reserves.

If we are digging for energy (oil, coal, uranium, etc.), *however*, we are limited economically by the amount of energy we can afford to expend to extract this new energy. From the point of view of the economy as a whole, there must be a net energy benefit; if there is not, no price can be high enough to make it economical. If, in order to tap new oil wells at the bottom of the sea, we use up the energy equivalent of a barrel of oil to find, extract, and distribute each barrel of oil to the ultimate user, there is no net energy benefit.

Cost calculations are made in dollars. The price of every item needed for the extraction process necessarily reflects the cost of the energy required to obtain the raw materials, process them, and combine them into the end product (the drilling rig, for instance). But a drilling operation can show a profit even though the economy suffers from a net energy loss, because much of the required energy was used to build the capital equipment years earlier at lower prices, and many costs, such as environmental pollution and disruption, are borne by the economy as a whole and are not charged to the operation. (These costs are ''externalized''.)

If oil is obtained from pools near the surface, the capital cost to locate the oil and drill the wells is low. The energy used to extract the oil and bring it to market is relatively small and the ratio of the energy obtained from the oil to the energy used to get it out is relatively high, sometimes as much as 9 : 1. But the deeper we go, the less net energy is obtained. If we have to drill in the Gulf of Mexico, for example, where the costs are much higher, the ratio may be as low as 3 : 1. It is, therefore, four times as expensive (9 less 1 = 8; 3 less 1 = 2). These are real costs and we all pay them. No wonder we have inflation.

These additional costs include the time, effort, and materials to build the giant drilling platforms and rigs needed in the Gulf, the extra equipment and people needed to service and maintain operations away from shore, and all the special collateral support facilities required.

The price mechanism is effective in balancing today's supply and demand. But it does not take the future into account, largely because individuals are seldom willing to pay extra money now for things they do not yet need. Even if you know that you will need 100 gallons of gasoline in 1986, and are sure it will cost you $5.00 a gallon then, you won't buy it now at today's market price and store it away. Our usual reaction is to let the future take care of itself; we have enough problems with today.

In the case of biological resources, there is the special danger that our ecological system is fragile. If we ignore its necessary balance, and push too hard to extract the utmost from one resource, we may destroy the system for all time.

In the living world, if a population of any species drops below a minimum, extinction follows. If a land is seriously overgrazed, it does not come back quickly, if at all. Much of the Sahara Desert and much of the barren lands of the Middle East were once fertile, until mankind ravaged and neglected them. If the vegetation that holds the topsoil is permitted to die, once the soil washes away there is no putting it back. The same is true of animal populations, from the smallest to the largest. Extinction becomes inevitable well before the number of individuals in the species gets down to two.

In the pursuit of whales, as an example, increased need for the products whales supply may result in the destruction of the very species upon which the whaling industry (now largely Japanese and Russian) depends. The industry has taken advantage of modern technology to become immensely efficient at catching the declining population of whales. There is no economic penalty preventing individual whalers from continuing inexorably to exterminate the whale population, because each feels that any whales he does not kill will be caught by his competitors instead. Since the whalers of no single nation own the oceans, no single nation or group has any economic incentive to harvest the crop in such a way that the breeding stock is protected, because its own restraint will merely permit the competition to catch more. No wise farmer would kill all his breeding bulls, if replacements were not available, yet each whaler, if he believes he should follow his own self interest as a good capitalist, would be remiss if he did not catch every possible whale as fast as he can before there are none left to catch.

The same economics applies to all ultimately finite resources. So long as petroleum is available, there is every incentive to bring it to market as fast as the market will take it. As drillers must go deeper and deeper to obtain it and as a growing proportion of the energy obtainable from the oil is needed to provide the equipment and energy to get it up, the yield declines and the cost escalates. But we will keep drilling until the day we find there is little or no net energy benefit at any price. We can only hope that we will have found adequate substitutes by then.

It is feasible to extract the tiniest fraction of a mineral from a mass of ore, provided available energy to do the extraction is unlimited. As the lodes become exhausted, we can work on poorer and poorer strata, provided a market exists at the higher price the extra costs of extraction will require.

Price adjustments, however, are useless in protecting against potential dangers to the total environment. Now that we are aware of air pollution, intense efforts are afoot to reduce it drastically or eliminate it entirely, and these programs should succeed, but not because of the operation of free enterprise capitalism. The polluter has little incentive to clean up his operation, unless someone forces him to do so. Regardless of the price he receives for his product, he is going to spend no more than he must to eliminate pollution.

If the pollution is not immediate and detectable, no one may be concerned until it is too late. We now know that DDT contamination of our rivers and lakes and of the oceans themselves will worsen for years, even if no more DDT is henceforth produced. The pesticide that has been spread on the land in the past quarter century is gradually being washed out of the soil, into the water table and eventually into the larger bodies of water. How serious that will be to mankind we don't yet know.

In our earliest concern over pollution problems, our first reaction was to attack symptoms rather than causes. Since then, considerable, although erratic, progress has been made toward improving our environment. The next few years will see more improvement. As the capitalist has little economic incentive to reduce or control pollution (air, water, noise or any other), this has been a proper area for government coercion, either by direct controls or by appropriate charges or taxes. (Wilfred Beckerman has made a good argument in favor of charges rather than controls.)[5]

Others who see no dangers in continued growth insist that the capacity of our world is not really limited. Capitalistic incentives, we are told, insure that hitherto unknown resources will be found that will supply whatever the demand may become. It is argued that, although we have no more geographical frontiers in which to expand, a host of technological frontiers still remain to be breached. Science and engineering will, it is said, come up with the answers to our needs as they arise.

This argument has been a good one, and history backs it. After all, the entire North American continent could support only a million or so Indians in prehistoric times. We have created great wealth from resources that were useless to our forebears; it is capitalism that made that possible. Immense further gains in the application of science to practical technology can be expected. As applied to our future, there is some truth in this argument, but it is based more on blind hope than on good evidence. Eventually, we come up against the intractable laws of physics—there will be no more to be had.

Since our whole world depends on energy to provide food, clothing, shelter, and all other material goods and services, the potential supply of energy will ultimately determine the rise or fall of our economy. In the last few years, we have become very aware of how much we depend upon the supply of hitherto cheap and plentiful fossil fuels to maintain our scale of living.

The need for greater productivity gets top attention from advocates of economic growth. A fundamental rule of capitalism is that its incentives promote the creation of greater total wealth so that there is more to distribute. The axiom is that increasing the total supply of goods and services is more beneficial to everyone than distributing present wealth more equitably. "Trickle down" economics really has worked.

When energy and material resources are limited, however, "productivity" needs careful redefinition. Increasing the amount produced by better techniques, better equipment, or smarter thinking is fine, provided no more energy or resources are used in so doing. If the same amount of goods is produced with less energy, we may have a saving. If we use the same energy in one aspect of our economy to produce more goods, our problem is that additional resources have been used to

19

provide the material for these extra goods. If, for instance, a maker of pots and pans improves the process so 150 instead of 100 are made every hour without using any more energy in the forming and polishing operations, to the extent that production is increased, it requires more metal, which itself took consider-able energy to find, extract, process and distribute. Inevitably, total energy consumption goes up.

Our dilemma is that freeing all the incentives of capitalism to work most effectively is the road to disaster in an energy-scarce world. We need those incentives badly, however, if we are to avoid stagnation and lethargy in a no-growth world. Can we reconcile the need for capitalist incentives and the impossibility of giving them free rein? That is what this book is about.

Assuming that population trends will continue pretty much as predicted, at least in the short run, certain important economic consequences may be expected. As energy becomes more ex-pensive, those activities which use large amounts of energy will be adversely affected. For instance, since it takes almost four times as much electrical energy per pound to manufacture aluminum as steel, the price of aluminum will rise dispropor-tionately unless and until more energy-efficient aluminum-making processes are adopted (or unless demand drops because the need for aluminum drastically declines).

The cost of energy and resources will begin to climb more rapidly than the price of labor. As our present trend continues, in the developed world, those companies, primarily large, which have invested vast sums in energy-intensive, labor-saving plants and equipment, will be at a disadvantage com-pared to others which have not automated so much and rely more on human labor, except where the automated methods are energy-efficient. The small company which hasn't been able to afford the ultimate in processing technology may be competitively better off in a future economy where human labor does some of the work which now requires massive inputs of energy power in automated plants. This will be a reversal indeed, which business economists have failed to anticipate.

Our capitalistic system is now programmed for trouble. We have been obsessed with the need for more automation of our industrial processes to reduce our dependence on human labor. Labor, however, no matter how high-priced it may seem, is increasingly abundant, while the materials and energy necessary to mechanize our lives are increasingly scarce. We have been going in exactly the wrong direction.

One astute commentator points out that it has been too easy in the past to equate progress with the wrong kind of growth:

> The corporations that were the most prosperous in the last 20 years were able to build the biggest most efficient labor-wise and most inefficient material-wise plants. But the cost of labor relative to materials is declining, so they are all wrong for the future.[6]

Many of our basic economic activities will have to be changed to become less energy-intensive. Businesses that were not able to afford automation so much as their competitors may be glad of that fact. Automation which requires high energy consumption may be priced out of the market.

We may expect a shift in American agricultural methods. The more intensively land is cultivated, the more expensive is each additional unit of product. When primitive humans first began to farm, it took little effort to collect the grain that weather and soil provided. Seeding and cultivating came later

21

and multiplied the yield; it also made them slaves to the soil.

Modern agriculture multiplies the farmer's productivity, but it requires intensive cultivation and heavy application of fertilizers. The energy cost represented by the operation of the farm machinery, plus the energy required to manufacture the equipment and mine, manufacture, and distribute the fertilizer, must in total be netted against the energy supplied by the food produced. By this criterion, the net energy per bushel of wheat produced by the poorest farmer in India with a bullock and wooden plow is greater than any grown in the United States, because of our gigantic energy input to obtain high yields per acre. Although yields per acre in the underdeveloped world are sometimes low by our standards, their agriculture is more efficient by all measures except in the amount of labor and land required.

American agriculture accounts for about 7% of our total fuel energy consumption, what with the enormous amount of energy required for gasoline and to extract, manufacture, and distribute fertilizer plus the amount represented in making and distributing farm machinery and equipment. As energy costs continue to rise in relation to labor costs, the economics of farming will change. I believe that our farm population is now near its all time low, and that there will be a gradual back-to-the-farm movement, not because of the bucolic charms of the country, but because farming will become more labor-intensive.

Warren A. Johnson has described some of the economic trends of the future that we may expect because of higher costs of energy.

Higher prices will not only discourage resource-intensive industries such as automobiles, air travel, construction, food processing, packaging and petrochemicals, but will also encourage the substitution of labor for material, which is just the opposite process that has occurred in the past as the relative cost of resources were declining compared to labor. We will see the remodeling of old houses gain at the expense of building new ones, the increased collection, sorting and reuse of scrap, and the squeezing out of two crops from fields where only one was grown before.[7]

Certain industries will be particularly hard hit. Capital goods industries are, by definition, growth-oriented. If your business is building electric power plants, every plant you build adds to the available power capacity. When our economy slows up, the construction industry will be particularly hard hit because we will need few new buildings of any kind, at least until present structures become unsuitable.

The effects on various industries will necessarily be uneven. Some companies will be badly hurt while others will thrive. Compensatory adjustments to level out the burden may prove impractical. Instead, we will have to hope for a gradual rolling change that will provide time for companies and individuals to adjust to the changing situation.

Glenn T. Seaborg agrees that there is no early or easy answer to the energy crisis. The recycle society, as he calls it, will develop an environmental and conservationist ethic due to the scarcity of resources as well as the new value placed on land, water, and air.

> We are accustomed to the ideas of unlimited growth from classical theories of economics, in which supply always rises to meet demand. But unlike capital, which is a construct of man, the natural resources of our earth are finite.[8]

Fuel energy and raw materials have not had unions to represent them and to struggle to push up their prices. We pay too little for potentially scarce energy and materials compared to the price of human labor. Low prices encourage us to use up energy and materials even to save insignificant amounts of human labor. We have also been encouraged to automate because machines are more obedient, more tractable, and generally give us less trouble than humans. We know how to manage machines; we have yet to learn how to work with our fellow humans.

Capitalism as we now know it can be adapted to a slower-paced economy only by avoiding several dilemmas.

First, capitalists must begin to recognize that we are approaching a steady-state no-growth economy, whether we like it or not. We must rid ourselves of the incubus of the growth mentality. If the business community can understand that growth is not a necessary prerequisite to business success, and that continued growth eventually will bring disaster, we will have made a long step forward.

We must start by facing up to the problem in our own individual businesses. "Growth" in the mindless sense in which it is used by businessmen, politicians, business economists, and the investment community must become a dirty word. I do not mean that I am opposed to all growth. Much of it is beneficial and necessary. It is growth for the sake of growth that we must abandon.

Second, we have to face up to the problem of unemployment. Our present economic and political system requires nearly full employment. In a slow-growth or no-growth society, the high cost of energy and resources will discourage the production of

24

non-essential goods that consume either of them. What do you do with people, if they can't make widgets? How do they live, if there is inadequate employment?

Whether we solve this problem by taking people off the labor market entirely or by using more human labor as a substitute for fuel energy, or by some other means, remains to be seen. I doubt that any single answer will be adequate. But we will have to eliminate the performance of energy-using jobs which do not clearly improve the quality of our lives; we will have little choice.

Third, we will have to develop effective incentives other than unlimited wealth and power to keep capitalism working. While I am far from an egalitarian, I see that the gross extremes of wealth and poverty must be changed. We will have to walk the tightrope of reducing disparities in wealth and income without destroying the incentives to excel. This may be our most difficult task.

If there is a way that capitalism can survive and even thrive in a steady-state economy, business executives should be interested. Once businessmen realize that they can make out pretty well in a no-growth society, they are less likely to fight to the end against every necessary adjustment in their way of life. Business people need not be dragged screaming into this strange new world. If we are to succeed in adapting to it, we need their brains, their abilities and their dedication.

My thesis is that capitalism can survive, even though with modifications, because growth is not integral to capitalistic success. Instead, smaller really is better—and often more profitable.

The thrust of this book is twofold:

1. To show why growth is not essential to business success, and that, in fact, smaller can often be more profitable.

2. To analyze the basic problems of capitalism in a slow-growth and no-growth society and suggest approaches that can keep it effective.

It is coincidence of sorts that this book has been written. My experience as a corporate manager has thrown me into a number of situations in which I found that a company had to be simplified and shrunk in size if it were to survive. In each case, the company not only survived, it prospered better than ever before with a smaller sales volume. I began to wonder why the results were so much better than were expected.

Although my experience as a corporate manager came first (and still continues), a lifelong interest in man's future as a species provided the background to undertake an intense study of the world picture as a whole. I was particularly concerned with the fields of population, resources, and energy. Only recently have my ideas in the fields of business and world problems converged.

This book draws upon my experience in the business world, pointing to reasons why thinking small is often better. In the decades ahead, which will involve the most profound changes in our economic system since the Industrial Revolution began, those businesses will do best which adapt most successfully to changing conditions. It will not be enough for a businessman to know all about his own particular industry; he will need to be fully aware of the long term trends that will change all our lives.

Businessmen, investors, and economists who rely solely on analysis of past trends and their extrapolation into the future are going to be badly led astray. Investment economists, in particular, seem to be blind. They would do better to buy some chickens and read the entrails. We are indeed on the verge of "one of the great discontinuities of human history,"[9] and all of us had best prepare for it.

Capitalistic enterprise can take directions which will protect it and preserve its values in times of change. Thinking small is one such direction. Businesses that remain flexible and maneuverable will win out. An understanding of some of the basic forces of our economic world will be necessary to select industry and product directions with the most promise.

It will be a fascinating period, provided we recognize both its perils and its opportunities. Businessmen have set much of the tone for our present civilization. Their intelligence, skill, and drive are vitally important if we are to adjust smoothly to changing circumstances.

In this book, I intend to show that the adjustments which are ultimately necessary for the economy as a whole can be good for capitalistic business, too. Until businessmen see how they can survive and thrive in a different kind of world, they cannot admit to themselves that undifferentiated growth can ever cease and see that it is wise for them to plan constructively for a less expansive world.

Change will be immensely difficult because it means reversal of some of our basic attitudes. But there is no choice. I have become convinced that the human species has already expanded too greatly in numbers and is using up our world resources too fast. I see little evidence that technology will come to the rescue in time to solve many of our problems, unless we recognize our limitations and adjust to them. Francis Bacon once said: "Man may command nature, but only by obeying her." We are just beginning to learn what this means.

2

The Disadvantages of Bigness

WE ARE SO ABSORBED in the necessity for growth that it scarcely ever occurs to us to look in any other direction for success. When a businessman has exploited as much of any particular market as he can reasonably expect to control, rather than settle for the tangible rewards which that market affords, he seeks new worlds to conquer. All of us seem desperately to fear stagnation, believing that there is no standing still, but only growth or shrinkage.

Failure to grow may, it is true, lead to disaster. In this rapidly changing world, there is no assurance that a product which now has a ready market will not soon be displaced by something newer and better. Since the best defense is supposed to be a good offense, aggressive efforts to expand are seen as the best way to shore up the business and insure its continued good health.

So automatically is it assumed that bigger is better, that business managers who are asked why they want to increase sales, acquire a new product line or another company, seem startled that the inherent virtue of what they propose should be questioned. They grope for good reasons such as "increased earnings" and "the strength of diversification." But the good reasons are almost always afterthoughts, because the real reason is "You gotta grow, don't you?"

Admittedly, standing still in the middle of a busy thoroughfare is dangerous. But that is not what I propose. Growth has its place; but so does shrinkage. Now let us constructively study operating our economy on a smaller scale.

What is growth? To a businessman, it means increases in sales, profits, and return on investment. To qualify as a growth company, these must increase at a greater rate than the economy as a whole. Although the businessman is principally concerned with the increase in profits, he often assumes that an increase in sales is the necessary antecedent. True, there is often a positive correlation between sales and profits, but it need not be so.

"Growth" has strong emotional connotations. Mere size is considered a measure of success. The man who heads the bigger business is almost automatically assumed to be the better businessman. He is rewarded with a higher salary, more perquisites, and, even in today's anti-business climate, more respect. Certainly he has more power, and power is an important source of ego-satisfaction. We businessmen tend, therefore, to enjoy growth for its own sake. We assume that growth is what makes capitalism go. We find it hard to imagine successful capitalism without it.

In our society as a whole, growth has several meanings. First, it refers to the increase in human population numbers; the U.S. population is now growing at about 0.7% per year (excluding immigration). Second, the best known measure of economic growth is Gross National Product (GNP). Third,

29

when GNP grows faster than population, increase in the per capita share of GNP is another kind of growth. The term "growth" is used in all these three senses.

What is good about growth? In the biological sense, every organism grows until it reaches maturity, at which point growth levels off and ceases. If life is good, then growth is good. But so is maturity. For the human being (as for almost all animal life), biological growth is merely a preparation for adult life and is not expected to continue indefinitely. Intangible growth, however, should continue throughout life—growth in knowledge and wisdom, growth in moral character, growth in ability and experience. These take the place of physical growth in our adult years.

In the corporate world, there is no such transition from one kind of growth to another. Corporations strive only to get bigger—and bigger—and bigger. This is what biologists call undifferentiated growth, which, like a cancer, feeds on itself.

When the United States was a thinly settled pioneer land, growth in numbers and growth in exploitation of the country's vast resources were obviously good. Free enterprise capitalism thrived in such an environment and prosperity followed. Today, however, our population has multiplied many times and crowded into our cities. Our use of energy per capita has climbed rapidly so that we are continuing to grow in all three ways. But it has not occurred to us to modify our formula for success. We still take our readings from the recent past. We ignore the evidence that the natural and world economic situations are changing in essential nature.

Economists for hundreds of years have expounded at length on the economies of scale. The United States has become a great nation partly because the scale of industrial operations made possible by the size of the market in its vast expanse justified automation to the nth degree, so that unit costs could be reduced to a minimum.

Economies of scale are easy to understand and usually apparent at a glance. Adam Smith's classic discussion "Of the division of labour" in the manufacture of pins in *The Wealth of Nations* is still valid. Modern industry has demonstrated that manufacture in large volume permits not only efficient divisions of labor, but the ultimate in automation.

In addition to the classic manufacturing economies of scale there are major marketing advantages to being big. Particularly in the consumer-product field, size is almost indispensable for obtaining adequate distribution. Massive, continuous advertising is necessary to get the customer's attention. The consumer has an attention threshold, and has to be told many times about a product before he or she notices it. Only the big company can afford to keep hammering the message home.

Besides, the very size of the marketing organization commands attention in the market place. Salesmen are everywhere, seeing that their products have the best positions on the shelves and that empty shelves are promptly replenished. When you are selling the housewife, bigness indeed pays well.

Perhaps most important, the large company has the financial power to restructure itself to its own benefit. It can take on bigger projects and assume greater risks without endangering its corporate health. Its size gives it political power which, carefully used, can enhance its competitive position. It has access to sources of funds, people, and information that the smaller company cannot afford.

Although the large company is a special target for the forces of anti-trust it has the resources to fight them effectively and hard. Sheer financial strength provides effective insulation permitting the large company to make its plans well ahead and stick to them even when times are difficult. In similar circumstances, smaller companies often must cancel their long-range programs in order to survive.

One major advantage of size is the financial clout to extract lower prices from suppliers, not because the supplier has significantly lower costs filling large orders, but because it is hungry for the boost to business that getting a large order can mean.

Electric power, for instance, is sold at lower rates to large users even though unit costs are almost the same for delivery to users of all sizes. Initially, a lower rate for a large user is economically justified because it costs less per kilowatt hour supplied to bring the power to such a consumer than to lay the cables to the vast number of individual homes that will, in the aggregate, use the same amount of electricity. Once the distribution network is built and paid for, however, power is a fungible commodity. The cost per watt is virtually the same whether you use one or a million kilowatts. True, there are more meter readings and billings to be made to the small user and there is more line leakage on many small lines than on one big one, but these are relatively minor cost differences. The financial statements of the large user reflect an economy of scale in purchases of large amounts of power, but the lower rate it pays is largely a benefit conferred because of its political strength, not an operating efficiency of large size.

Financial power takes many forms. Sheer size brings a kind of muscle that can be used not only to buy at lower prices, but to obtain special privileges and options and sell more effectively and aggressively. It takes careful individual analysis to determine how much the large organization is truly benefiting from economies of scale and how much from use of its position to obtain special advantages.

The growth of the conglomerate companies in the nineteen sixties was first hailed as proof of the benefits of centralized control and management. In fact, the presumed economies of scale of conglomerate management did not exist, but were actually reflections of financial power in a rising market. Now we can see this.

In summary, therefore, there are economies of scale primarily in direct manufacturing plus some in the distribution and financial area. But they are not so great as they seem, because the advantages of bigness often come from the application of corporate muscle rather than from true economies of scale.

While we hear much about the so-called advantages of great size, there has been little thought about the disadvantages of bigness, which economists call the *diseconomies of scale*. Since World War II, increased automation has steadily reduced the proportion of blue collar workers in the total work force. At the same time, the increasing complications of corporate control and management have forced a disproportionate increase in administrative and clerical functions.

Automation of production operations sharply reduces the need for production workers. In some fully automated operations, such as some chemical-processing plants, the need for direct laborers to perform operations in the process itself may be eliminated entirely.

But overhead costs have *not* come down; in fact, they have usually climbed. Automatic machinery is expensive to buy, run, and maintain. That means higher depreciation costs, greater electric power and more machinery maintenance expense.

Sophisticated operations and controls require more high paid skilled technicians and executives. In addition, in today's business climate, a large executive and clerical staff must cope with hundreds of government regulations, file necessary reports and supervise required operational changes. This costs money, lots of it. Running a business today is many times more complex a task than even twenty years ago.

Accounting, even with the best of tools, is more art than science. Getting a clear picture of how a business is doing is not easy. In the manufacturing business, for instance, it is hard to determine what individual product costs really are. Because there is no single correct way of measuring and allocating overhead costs among different corporate activities, accountants look for shortcuts to understanding. Sometimes these rules of thumb lead us astray.

One such rule of thumb was popular not long ago. Burden rate used to be considered a measure of manufacturing efficiency. I can remember manufacturers in the late forties and early fifties saying proudly: "My factory burden [manufacturing overhead] rate is *only* 100% [or whatever it was]."

"Manufacturing burden" is a ratio between two figures: manufacturing overhead expense and direct labor expense. Reducing overhead expenses was once considered a most important task, and a low burden rate meant that overhead costs were being kept low. But, like any ratio, changes can be made in either or both figures which make it up. A highly automated plant operated by a very few laborers will have a high burden rate (1000% or more), because the bottom figure in the ratio is so small. In a modern fully automated plant with zero direct labor, the burden rate is infinite, because, although the bottom figure is zero, there is always some overhead; thus burden rate as a measure of efficiency becomes largely meaningless.

But other rules of thumb are still used. Standard accounting systems are not designed to reflect the inefficiencies and confusion of increasing complexity. Overhead expenses, including general, administrative, and selling expenses, need to be allocated to different product groups if we are to know all the costs each product line incurs. In their analysis of the corporation, managers struggle to assign as much as possible of the total overhead expense directly to product lines so they can tell what product costs are. Many of the activities being examined, however, involve general operations of the total business, often too complex to be worth the detailed analysis that is necessary for specific allocation to particular products. As a result, overhead tends to be allocated to all product lines in proportion to sales volume (or manufacturing cost of sales).

Old and new product lines tend to be charged the same proportionate rate for overhead, even though the newer lines incur far greater costs to get them started. The new product line that adds one more straw to the management load rarely gets charged as much as it should, while the well-established line which runs itself is expected to carry the overhead load for the new line. The extra costs of greater size and complexity are buried and not identified.

A few years ago a company I headed disposed of a line of portable positive displacement pneumatic machines which we had built to an annual sales volume of about $500,000. Although the line was a natural companion to our much larger, long established line of fan-operated equipment and we had devoted prodigious effort to get it going, it had not made money and the prospects of success were poor. We finally made the painful decision to sell the line for a nominal amount. The buyer was one of our employees who made it his own business, which later proved modestly successful.

The beneficial effects of the sale on our operation were substantial and almost instantaneous. Our balance sheet improved dramatically overnight as we collected the remaining accounts receivable, worked off the inventory, and, by buying no more material, cut our accounts payable. Our earnings improved more than the elimination of this relatively minor line seemed to justify. Only then did we realize how much this one activity had demanded in attention and effort from almost everyone in the company which could then be redirected to do a better job in our main programs. The books of account, however, had given us only a hint that this might be the happy result.

Cost accounting is, at best, an inexact study, with limited goals. It is a way of looking at the costs attributable to a particular product or activity to compare it with other activities of the company.

Several cost accounting techniques effectively hide diseconomies of scale in corporations. One of these is marginal-income accounting. Much has been written about the advantages of marginal income. The theory is that, for a short period, additional sales can be added to normal sales volume and be profitable even at prices that do not cover a proportionate share of fixed overhead, because 100% of the fixed overhead of the company is presumed to be borne by the regular business anyway. Accepting business at a price which does not cover a full share of overhead is dangerous, however.

Overhead is rarely as fixed as accountants are inclined to think, except for very short periods. In any long-range analysis of a business, there is no such thing as fixed overhead—it is all variable to some degree, even such items as rent, heat, light and power, depreciation and amortization, professional services and executive salaries.

Except for rare and well-controlled exceptions, marginal business taken to keep the operation going incurs the same overhead costs as the regular business and, by adding to the complexity of the total operation, often requires more than normal overhead. If the overhead really cannot be cut during a short period of overcapacity, it may make sense to take business at prices that will pay less than full overhead expenses, because a modest contribution to paying these expenses may be better than none. The danger is that an emergency measure often becomes standard practice; that is a good way to go broke.

Marginal-income accounting in one company may create a false economy of scale in another. In the scramble to sell the giant customer, manufacturers take a marginal-income approach to pricing in competing for its business, hoping to make up in volume what they lose in unit price. In the long run, they rarely succeed, but the big user benefits from an apparent but unreal economy of scale, by being able to purchase his needs at a bargain price.

Breakeven accounting is another management tool which inadvertently encourages growth for growth's sake. As with marginal income accounting, the theory is that certain elements of overhead cost vary with the volume of operations while others, deemed "fixed costs," do not. The sale price is set to provide for material, labor costs, and variable overhead costs plus an additional increment to allow for fixed overhead costs and profit. When the shipments are high enough in a given period to absorb all variable costs plus the total lump of fixed overhead costs, one has reached the breakeven point. The margin above variable costs on additional shipments goes entirely to profit, because all the fixed overhead costs have already been fully taken care of. No wonder a manufacturer gloats about a high volume month: although he makes no money and actually loses until the volume reaches the breakeven level, his profit on volume above the breakeven point is disproportionately large.

The fallacy of breakeven accounting is the assumption that expenses are easily divisible into fixed and variable. Except in the very short run, there really are few, if any, fixed expenses. If you lease a 100,000 square foot plant for a 10 year term, cost accountants will normally treat your rent as a fixed expense. But is it really? If you don't have enough space, you can rent more and thus increase that expense. If you have too much space, you can sublet part of the space, or, if that is impractical, you can even buy your way out of the lease and move to a smaller building. Rent expense can vary up or down.

The danger is that we tend to pay no attention to so-called fixed expenses, and just live with them. Even worse, we assume that we are stuck with them and must increase volume as the only means to pay for them.

One able executive of a large merchandising company recently was quoted as saying: "Our biggest problem is sales. Our industry has high fixed costs, and we have to promote hard to maintain a rate of sales sufficient to cover these costs. Securing more sales is far and away our No. 1 problem."[1] This is a typical business attitude which assumes that the cost structure is a given and the company must grow in order to cover all the overhead.

One common method of costing is a variation of breakeven accounting. Manufacturers often take their profits only at the tail-end-of-a-run, absorbing all their fixed overhead on the entire project before any profit is counted. In airplane manufacture, for instance, it is common to determine how many planes must be sold before the company breaks even. This stimulates concern principally with the volume of sales, not with margins, because once the fixed costs have been absorbed, profits on the last increment of volume (either monthly, or, if it is a one-shot product, by unit) are big, encouraging the attitude that more is automatically better.[2]

It is understandable that accounting practice permits amortization of much of the fixed costs of a project (particularly tooling and start-up costs) over the estimated number of units expected to be produced. Management may hedge against the unpleasant necessity of taking a big writeoff of unamortized costs if the product doesn't sell well by planning for sales of a low number of units. The major emphasis is on marketing effectiveness rather than cost effectiveness. Therefore, the goal is to get rid of as many units as possible, whether the market needs them or not. In view of this, it is not surprising that increasing sales is generally the accepted prescription for corporate ills.

Allocation of costs to product lines based on manufacturing cost of sales, marginal-income accounting, breakeven accounting and tail-end-of-the-run accounting all make the assumption that overhead costs include certain "fixed" costs that the company has to pay regardless of whether it is running at capacity or is totally idle. If we recognize that all overhead expenses are variable (although a few take time and effort to change) it is easier to identify the costs which can be eliminated by trimming the organization down in size and complexity.

As operations grow larger and more complex, overhead tends to increase as a percentage of costs. At the management level, there are few economies of scale. In fact, above the direct labor level, small is generally better and more efficient. Doubling the number of people or products to be controlled more than doubles the costs and difficulties of control itself. For the same reason, when sales volume drops significantly for an extended period of time (and not just for a month or so), it is possible to reduce overhead even more than proportionately.

Why is this so? What are some of the major diseconomies of scale? In the corporate world, they appear in a number of disguises.

Cumbersome size is a major handicap of large corporations. It has become a truism that a small company can run circles around a giant competitor, because it is able to react so much faster to changes in conditions. One important reason is that small businesses enjoy better internal communications.

The ineffectiveness of communications in large organizations is probably the most important single diseconomy of scale. As the scale of operations increases, communication becomes more difficult for two prime reasons: 1) increasing distances between activities; 2) increasing numbers of channels necessary for communication.

The increasing distance is not merely geographical (after all, the telephone gives us speed-of-light communication). But the manager of a large company lives in a different world from most of his workers and speaks a different language. The larger the organization the less contact there is between manager and worker. No wonder that they often fail to understand each other.

An equal problem is the sheer number of necessary contacts. In a business with 1,000 employees, even though not every employee needs to communicate with each of the other 999, they tend to establish a vast number of channels, formal and informal. While the number of people increases arithmetically, the variety of contacts grows geometrically (exponentially). Thus, when there are two people involved, there is only one channel of communication between them. When the number doubles to four, the channels climb from one to six. (Look at ⊶ compared to ⊠ .) By the time the number reaches eight, if each of the eight deals with all the other seven, there are a total of twenty-eight channels of communication. (Any electrician who attempts to do the wiring to connect more than three switches to one light has experienced this).

The standard organization chart is an attempt to organize the necessary contacts in a business. It is an upside-down tree which provides for messages from the root (at the top of the trunk) down the branches through all the levels to the twigs.

Presumably, the messages along the communication channels can go both ways. Often, they don't even go one way, because of blocks and distortions en route. Have you ever played the game in which an anecdote is passed secretly from person to person around a circle? If so, you know that the original message is usually almost unrecognizable after half a dozen repetitions. Imagine, then, what happens to information traveling up or down a corporate chain of command, particularly when it intimately affects the business lives of the transmitting individuals.

Fortunately, the organization chart doesn't tell the whole story, although it helps prevent utter confusion as corporate size increases. The normal organization chart is a gross simplification of the actual channels. An informal chart would have to show more threads than a spider web. The bigger the company, the more the crosslinkages, not to mention the necessary detours to get around those who fail to communicate. Don't forget the rumor grapevine, which often gets the word first.

In one important sense, management is a communications network. Because human communications are slow and faulty, the economies of large-scale production in the factory are often offset by the diseconomies of scale in the hierarchy necessary to direct its extensive operations.

Many middle managers act primarily as telephone exchanges, receiving and sorting messages and retransmitting them. The input which each provides in doing his job is, in itself, based largely on knowledge and experience in the job and obtained by education programmed into him either at school or from his superiors.

I am not derogating the middle manager's skill and ability. I have been both a middle manager and a foreman, and I know it is not easy, but that is not the point. His job is still primarily one of expediting the communications made necessary by the scale of the operation. As the scale of the enterprise increases, the manager can no longer know personally everything that happens, but must rely on others to keep him informed. When the business is large, communication is expensive and slow and, therefore, inefficient.

Good communications are really the essence of management. Productivity will drop when communications are lacking, whether the organization is large or small.

Communications are often unappreciated until you try to function without them. In India, the caste system (legally dead but still dominant) inhibits good communications because people in a higher caste traditionally want no contact with the lower castes. The lower castes are unclean—one does not talk to any of them or even take notice that they exist. In an Indian household, the domestic help drift in, drift out. Presumably the work gets done, eventually.

A caste system that worked tolerably well for centuries in a small, simple society cannot be transferred to a large modern industrialized society without drastic changes. Such a system is particularly vulnerable as an organizational entity because of the absence of intercaste communications.

Indian industrial leaders have recognized this. In heavy industry, such as steel mills, modern management techniques have been imposed. They recognize that complicated coordination of industrial processes cannot be dependent upon casual decisions of the individual worker as to whether he comes or goes, pulls this lever or that, or takes a nap by his machine. When the benefits of economy of scale are sought, if chaos is to be avoided, the caste system must be suppressed.

American managers are often just as poor at communications without the history of the rigid caste system. We tend to know all the words, but don't seem to be able or to want to apply them.

Management consultants have made fortunes from the inability or unwillingness of managers to find out what is going on in their own businesses. Once the management consultant has obtained the contract to review and advise a company on management organization and practices, his first move will be to learn as much as possible about the present organization. A proper technique is to interview a substantial number of employees at various levels in the hierarchy to find out how the organization is supposed to work and how it actually does.

Often the lower level workers have an intelligent and intimate knowledge of facets of the business that managers don't know, and the wise consultant soon finds this out and makes good use of it. The manager may not think his own people are capable of solving the problem. (''Who else loused it up so that we have to change?'') But if the managers don't think the workers know what is wrong, it is probably because they have never really tried to find out from them. Consultants are expert at picking the brains of second- and third-level employees, and feeding their findings back to management as their own brilliant ideas. The result: the employees feel cheated that outsiders have been paid to report what they would gladly have told, had management really shown some interest in their opinions. Next time, they'll tell even less.

Communication in larger organizations tends to be more remote and impersonal and therefore less effective. Morale is harder to maintain when the chain of command is long. Business communication must be both factual (what needs to be done and how to do it) and emotive (stimulating the desire to perform). Emotive communication, in particular, has to be reasonably direct to be effective at all.

In small organizations, communication can be largely oral. Policies can be developed on the spot or modified at will to deal with special situations. In the big company, everything must be written. Procedures are needed to cover every conceivable personnel contingency in advance, lest unfortunate precedents be set. These policies have to be rigidly applied to all personnel, with little room for consideration of individual problems. Some managers, it is true, may believe it is an advantage to have all such matters cut and dried. It may make management seem easier, but it does not make it more effective.

The number of transactions in a business in itself creates another diseconomy of scale. In day-to-day operations of a business, for instance, memory for numbers and letter combinations is invaluable: model numbers, part numbers, prices, and other designations. Since computers use only binary numbers (which they translate into decimal numbers), as the scale of operations has required increasing computerization, decimal numbers have tended to replace letters or number-letter combinations. Since there are only 10 digits (compared to 10 digits plus 26 letters) from which to make combinations, part numbers and other codes tend to be longer and therefore harder to remember.

Today, when you leave your telephone number with someone's secretary so that person can call you back, how many secretaries can write down the seven numbers correctly if you give the number only once? My experience is: not many. The two letters and four numbers for telephone numbers in the less-crowded world of a generation ago were far easier to remember.

The loss of autonomy when small units join large organizations is another major diseconomy of scale. Shortly after World War II, businessmen began to talk about the advantages of local autonomy in running multiplant operations. They saw that the span of command of an individual manager was effective in inverse proportion to the number of people under him. The fewer he bossed, the more thoroughly and effectively he could control them.

Somehow the computer changed this. In the early years, computers were so expensive that they could be used only for large operations. If we were to make effective use of the computer to control our operations we had to centralize. Since few people were good computer programmers, and the earlier generation machines had little or no built-in programming, we had to centralize all computer operations in one place, rather than have separate systems for each operating unit. Thus we made business fit the computer, rather than vice versa. All this encouraged bigness and complexity of systems. Although computers are far more flexible and far less expensive today, we still tend to make man fit the machine rather than the machine fit man.

If a company had ten plants making much the same product each for a different geographical region, it was assumed that centralizing many of the functions at a headquarters office made economic sense, because one good control system for all plants could be developed, using only the best personnel to pull everything into line.

It is not so simple. Over the years, different systems will have developed in the different plants, partly because of different conditions and problems, but also because different managers work differently. Reconciling them all to one functional control system may cause monstrous problems. In the process, control may be lost entirely.

Consider the case of the branch plant with the lazy purchasing agent. His suppliers' salesmen regularly do his job by checking his inventory in his warehouse and telling him what he needs to order and when. The system works. But once the purchasing job is centralized, the main purchasing department has to have its own central inventory control system connected with all plants. If that system is ever in error, there is no routine feedback to warn the company that they may be in trouble, until shipment has to be made and the bins are found empty. Centralization can work, but it requires smarter and more energetic and alert people to avoid disruptions.

For a generation the mystique of the computer blinded us to the inefficiencies of great size. As we move on to the fourth, fifth, and umpteenth generation of computers, we will find that this marvelous tool will be valuable in at least two directions: 1) to enable us to make immense progress in solving the incredibly complex systems problems in economics, sociology and biology which we have only dimly understood so far, and 2) to give small operations the same kinds of real time information at reasonable cost that have helped the big organizations (private and public) offset some of the built-in diseconomies of scale.

Running a small business is inherently more difficult than managing a giant corporation. The problem is that the small businessman must be personally well grounded in all aspects of business operation. He cannot afford specialists on his payroll who have become trained experts each in a limited area of responsibility. But the small businessman has the offsetting advantage of instant control over the operation of his business so that he can react promptly to changes in his market. He may be largely unaware of what is happening outside his own business, but his modest scale of operations doesn't require the massive planning and preparations that the large organization must make far in advance of any significant change. He can and does shoot from the hip quite effectively.

Big organizations are complex and the complexity increases geometrically (exponentially), while size increases arithmetically (e.g., twice as big is four times as complex).

Peter Drucker compares the corporation with an organism:

> It is a biological law that the larger an organization grows the greater is the ratio between its mass and its surface, the less exposure to the outside there is for the cells on the inside. As living organisms grow they therefore have to develop special organs of breathing, perspiration and excretion. It is this law

that sets a limit to the size of living organisms, . . . ; and the business enterprise stands under this law as much as any other organism.[3]

Apply this distinction between linear and cubic measure to a simple case. Assume a source of objectionable noise such as an airplane engine. If the level of noise is doubled, since it radiates noise in all directions, the space in which its effect is objectionable is expanded to double the former radius from the source. If the noise was objectionable for a distance of 2000 feet before, it would now be too noisy at 4000 feet distance. But a sphere with a radius of 4000 feet is eight times as big as one with a 2000-foot radius, so that the doubling of the noise increases the scope of the problem eight times. If we are concerned only with the land area affected, it has gone up four times. Of course, if, instead, the noise is halved in volume, the improvement is equally dramatic.

Casualty insurance companies are beginning to learn that there is more than twice as much exposure in providing liability insurance for a 200,000-ton oil tanker, for instance, than for a 100,000-ton ship, even though the former costs less than twice as much to build (and costs scarcely any more to operate), because the potential damage from a loss that would dump 200,000 tons of oil into the ocean at one time is far more than twice that from 100,000 tons.

The damage done by the oil from the 120,000-ton *Torrey Canyon,* which sank in the English Channel in 1967, seemed immense at the time. That was, however, just a first glimpse of the problem to come. Until the *Torrey Canyon* sank, most previous oil dumpings seemed to have been absorbed by the ocean without notable adverse effect. But the *Torrey Canyon* breakup was big and concentrated enough so that the threshold was passed, with devastating effect on fish, bird, and marine life in the vicinity of the disaster.[4]

When a World War II light bomber collided with the Empire State Building more than a quarter century ago, little damage was done except to the plane and its occupants. Can you imagine the holocaust that would now occur if a giant 747 jetliner were to fall in any crowded city and catch fire? Beyond the loss of the lives of passengers and crew, the intense heat would spread far wider and would thus multiply the property damage far out of proportion to the relative sizes of the 747 and those smaller earlier planes. Such a loss would be so catastrophic that any insurance company that accepted the entire risk could be severely hurt.

Bigness also means complexity. In some areas of activity, there is no choice but to be big. Obviously, the most efficient sizes for steelmills and for popcorn wagons are different. We should recognize, however, that we pay a price for technological bigness in actual diseconomies of scale.

The Saturn V rocket, which took the astronauts into space in the Apollo program, weighed over six million pounds. It consisted of more than a hundred thousand parts, many of them incredibly complex in themselves. So critical was the importance of most of these parts, that success of the mission required almost 100% reliability performance. To be sure that none of this vast assemblage of parts would fail, a higher level of manufacturing quality than ever before required was obligatory for all components.

If there are ten parts in a product and the failure of any one will cause total failure, then one needs to be almost 99% certain that each part is non-defective, to have a 90% chance that the produce will succeed. If the product contains one hundred parts instead of ten parts, then one needs 99.89% reliability for each part to have the same 90% overall chance of success.[5] If there are 100,000 critical parts, and when a 90% chance of success is not good enough, quality standards must be much more stringent. The requirement of virtual perfection in component manufacture multiplied the cost of the Apollo moon program several times, because each part had to be so overbuilt that failure would be all but impossible. (The rocket can fulfill its mission even if certain parts fail, because redundancy is designed and built-in at extra cost as one method of protecting against almost inevitable failure of a few components. But most systems cannot be duplicated without making the rocket so heavy it cannot get off the ground.)

We have become so accustomed to the gradual growth of our technological society that we are scarcely aware of its interlocking complexity and the utter dependence of each activity upon all those other activities with which it interacts.

One price of bigness is the necessity for near-perfection in all the elements that make it up. While centralized control makes a tight discipline possible, it is only as good as the people who direct it. To the extent that responsibility can be removed from fallible humans and invested in automatic machinery, the problems of human inadequacy can be reduced. But even machines, designed and built by humans, fail.

The idolatry of gigantism is the core of modern business management. Most of the best and brightest business school graduates go to work for the biggest companies. Big business needs them; without the keenest and most alert brains, it would collapse in confusion.

The disadvantages of great size and complexity apply to any

organizational structure. Management of the operation, whether it is a manufacturing corporation, a marketing network, a college or university or a government agency, becomes more difficult as it gets bigger.

Excessive size is, indeed, a disease of our civilization. We are enchanted with bigness without realizing the price we pay for it. It is time we looked closer.

3

Vulnerability of Large Size

"THE BIGGER THEY ARE, THE HARDER THEY FALL!" may have been coined as a battle cry to improve morale when tackling a large opponent. In our technological world, however, it has a special truth.

As our numbers grow and we have to depend more on technology to keep things running, our civilization becomes more vulnerable to breakdowns. The very success of capitalistic enterprise in finding technological solutions to our increasing problems breeds more dependence and more vulnerability. The bigger and better we get, the more precariously we live.

Any large interdependent structure is susceptible of disruption in direct proportion to its technological sophistication. When something goes wrong in one place the failure tends to propagate through the whole network. The effective operation of the system is dependent on everything working right; one or two simultaneous failures at critical spots can cause total collapse. The system may be a large company, an electric power network or a whole economy. In a relatively primitive society, as in most less developed countries, a temporary failure of electric power causes little inconvenience. On the contrary, in our developed world, it can be catastrophic.

In *The Coming Dark Age*,[1] Roberto Vacca describes dramatically how a simple combination of highway and railway traffic tieups could initiate a sequence of events that would rapidly paralyze our whole economy and end in an immense number of deaths. The more complex our technological interrelationships become, the more likely is total collapse. It is a frightening prospect. By contrast, the relatively simple (and localized) societies of the underdeveloped world are largely immune to this kind of technological collapse because their systems are not sophisticated enough to be interdependent.

We become aware of our vulnerability when a strike by some small group (the sewage plant workers, the bridge tenders or the telephone-maintenance workers) strangles a city so that all production activity is gradually brought to a halt. Or, if a critical machine breaks down, such as a computer that handles airline reservations, chaos can ensue, because humans can no longer keep track of the rapid adjustments the system requires. It is too complex and too big.

An explosion, a landslide, or a hurricane can cause far greater damage today not only because we live in a so-much-more crowded world, but particularly because of our dependence on the uninterrupted operation of our complex interlocking technological system. A monkey wrench in the works can be devastating now. In an article in *Harper's Magazine*, Martin Koughan predicts what might happen in a certain large city when an earthquake next occurs (''Goodbye, San Francisco'', August, 1975). Most cities don't share this particular vulnerabilty, but there are many other roads to collapse. Can we forget that we can almost count on one or more nuclear disasters somewhere in the world in the next decade or two, now that a vast number of people have access to the knowledge and materials needed to make an atomic bomb at low cost?

Our security requires greater self sufficiency of the units of our economy, whether businesses or communities. A ship is divided into watertight compartments so that damage can be sustained in one area without sinking the ship. We provide for emergency generating plants for hospitals and a few other major installations to take over if the main electric network fails. Picture what would happen if the food supply or the water supply were shut off for merely a week in any large city. Our systems just have to keep on working; there is no alternative.

Compartmentalizing our economy makes good sense. Any damage control expert will tell you that the first step is to reduce the scope of the danger by keeping it small. Why else do the fire insurance people insist on impermeable firedoors dividing large buildings into separate units?

Even without the intervention of outside force, the system can easily collapse from its own inefficiency and confusion. Large organizations are far from superhuman. They tend to drift out of control.

In any large organization, business or governmental, the purposes of the organization as a whole get lost in the workings of bureaucracy. People are assigned certain jobs to do. If they are more than one or two echelons below the top, adequate performance of the specific task becomes an end in itself, regardless of how it relates to total organizational goals. You do your job, and whether or not it truly contributes to the whole is immaterial to you.

Any organization becomes a bureaucracy to the extent that

the individual members believe that they will advance their own interests best by playing politics with their associates and superiors rather than by forwarding the purposes of the organization. By this definition, many large companies have clearly become bureaucracies. In small companies, bureaucracy can develop, but individual visibility is so high that it is quite rare except where management is incompetent or blind.

I have seen this in large corporations. When I was active in the manufacture of aerospace components sold to the large airplane and rocket engine manufacturers, I had many insights into how a big company works (or fails to work). We dealt with the middle echelons of these companies—the engineers, the quality control men, and the buyers. Rarely did one encounter any real concern for the success of the program as a whole— each person wanted only to keep his own nose clean by having the paperwork show that his record was clear, regardless of cost.

In one instance, we manufactured a number of parts which proved to be totally useless, because of an error in the specifications the customer supplied to us. Rather than admit error to the appropriate government agency, our customer rebuilt all of the parts to the correct specification at more than twice the cost of buying a set of replacement parts from us. After all, only the taxpayer was hurt.

In a large corporation, it is almost impossible to avoid an impersonal atmosphere because of its sheer size. The same is even more true in a population as a whole. The small independent community, social, economic, or political, needs little formal government. As numbers and technology increase arithmetically, the complexity increases geometrically. The modern city, for instance, requires the efficient coordination of the specialized activities of countless people and machines to function at all. Some scarcely do.

The same indifference is now apparent in the average citizen's attitude toward his government. Although there are probably many causes, an important one must be our feeling of remoteness from its workings. Government has become something alien, not a part of us. It no longer seems to be an extension of our own community. We turn our backs on it, by seeking security on our own, wearing blinders. If we can't see evil, it doesn't exist. We don't want to become involved.

Nor do we trust our servants in government any longer; in our giant world, they are remote and faceless. The term "servants" seems laughable today, even though we have the illusion that we elect them. Even in the local community, there are so many more people than in earlier days that we all feel anonymous. Each of us is so small a part of the whole that, more than ever before, our concern is with our own special problems to the virtual exclusion of matters of general import.

High morale can exist in large organizations, of course, and some nourish it well. It takes more skill, however, to attain good morale on a large scale. I maintain that the art of management is in getting average people to do a top job. When the organization is large and complex, it takes better than average people to get the results you need. Where contact between worker and management is frequent and close, it is much easier. Small size doesn't guarantee more worker interest in company objectives, but it certainly improves the chances of achieving it.

The benefits of smallness can be achieved inside large organizations. Many big businesses have successfully minimized the diseconomies of scale by breaking up the organization into a number of discrete semi-autonomous units.

Vulnerability of Large Size

Once when we were trying to sell a manufacturing operation, the corporate development officer of one of the leading conglomerate companies visited our facilities. After a day's study, he reported that they were interested in buying our total company, but not just the two thirds of it that we wished to sell, because separating our different operations would cause them accounting problems they did not want to undertake. They had such a tiny corporate staff that they discouraged any of their subsidiaries from doing business with any of the others because of the intracorporate accounting problems that would be created. As a result, their various subsidiaries were almost completely isolated from one another. The parent company was uninterested in "synergy," the catchword of the merger age. I remember thinking that their unwillingness to supervise their subsidiaries was very amusing. Maybe so—but I note that they have thrived while other brighter stars have dimmed.

They let autonomy really work—and it does. Owning stock in such a conglomerate has a number of benefits:

1 The total company is large enough to require a large stock issue with lots of stockholders and a highly marketable stock.
2 Risks of the subsidiaries that do well are averaged with those of the ones that don't.
3 The benefits of smallness are retained because of the autonomous management of each subsidiary.

In view of the present legal and tax structure of our economy, this is one way the investor can find the advantages of liquidity and smallness in one stock. The disadvantage is that he cannot select which subsidiaries to back; he takes the good with the bad.

One giant food and drug conglomerate has done outstandingly well, at least partly because it allows its many subsidiaries to run themselves without interference; but if the subsidiary doesn't perform as well as the parent believes it should, the subsidiary is promptly sold.

A major diseconomy of the scale of our total numbers comes from crowding. The sheer mass of human numbers affects everything we do. While neither large nor small businesses escape the effects of a crowded society, the greater diseconomies are experienced by those with the most widespread activity. As urbanization pulls more and more of us into city centers, the higher speeds of transportation between cities are more than offset by the traffic congestion and delays at the journey's beginning and end.

Employees who must commute to work in or near the cities of today know how costly it is in time, money and nervous energy just to get to the job and home again when the day is over. The conscious self becomes accustomed to losing an hour or two or three a day in bucking traffic. The body obeys the will, but the stresses build up subconsciously and often erupt in the form of bad temper, illness, or even premature death. Those who live near their work or can commute quickly by public transportation are indeed fortunate.

There is a threshold effect which aggravates the problems of crowding. A sewage system designed for a city of 10,000 people works well until the population gets a little too large, then it breaks down all at once. When a highway is designed for 5,000 cars an hour, if 7,000 or 8,000 cars try to use it, traffic comes almost to a halt. When a telephone switchboard is overloaded for an extended period of time so that calls cannot be promptly placed, the need to place calls a number of times to get through once crowds the circuits even more, and in so doing makes the situation even worse.

The self-sustaining nuclear reaction, which gives us both power and the bomb, is the most dramatic example of a threshold effect. The nuclear chain reaction depends on achieving a certain critical mass of radioactive material in precisely limited space, at which point the reaction becomes self-generating and self-sustaining. Until the material is packed close enough to reach this critical point, the individual radioactive particles decay slowly without bringing on any major changes in the environment. Beyond that limit, nuclear fission begins, with all its attendant effects.

Corporations have threshold problems, too, and mere size breeds them. Once a company becomes large enough to be well known, it receives far more attention from the public, the media, and a host of government agencies. Some of this attention may be welcome, but most of it is not. The top officers of the company spend much of their time dealing with problems with which the small businessman has little concern.

For example, legal problems mount disproportionately. There is a legal saying: *De minimis non curat lex*, which, freely translated, means the law does not concern itself with trifles. Legal matters that could be treated casually if the company were small have to be dealt with meticulously (and expensively) merely because the magnitude of the operation exposes the company to many threats or mischances which now represent large dollar amounts.

All kinds of decisions become more difficult because of company size. Laying off six hundred people is news; sixty is not. If the company is a major factor in the economy, it is subjected to public pressure. Giant steel and aluminum companies get jawboned about prices and wages; the local machine shop is ignored. The small organization has much more freedom of maneuver because it is little noticed by the government and the public.

If the company becomes publicly owned, its problems mount. It is subject to extensive regulation by the Securities and Exchange Commission. The intense spotlight on its every move makes rapid decisions impossible and most risky decisions inadvisable. No wonder the small company can usually run circles around the big one.

Recently, a company I know was required to file a complex S2 registration with the SEC in order to acquire an agricultural cooperative which has less than 100 shareholders. A massive prospectus to inform these shareholders was finally found acceptable to the government, after endless changes and several months' delay. The cost was about $150,000 in legal fees and printing expenses. Somewhere, an original good reform idea for securities regulation got smothered in paperwork and verbiage. I doubt whether any person learned anything from the final document that would have modified the opinion he obtained from the preliminary draft.

Bureaucrats (like authors) get infatuated with their own words. When authors are too wordy, they don't get printed; but bureaucrats tend to be held in higher esteem, the more paperwork tonnage they can generate. And lawyers, who write most of our laws, get paid by the hour for interpreting them.

Mere physical bigness brings its own problems. Casualty-insurance companies may be expected to have an increasingly tough time getting rate increases fast enough to cover bigger and wider exposures in a more-crowded world in which accidents or destructive weather, wherever they occur, are much more apt to hit people or their property than in a sparsely settled world.

In a modern skyscraper, the danger is that the more-complicated mechanisms required to keep it functional are more subject to breakdown and sabotage. (You don't need elevators in a two story building.) There is a particular exposure to calamitous damage from fire (popularized in a recent movie thriller), because the best fire fighting equipment is ill adapted to coping with blazes in high buildings. Bigger is indeed more vulnerable and riskier.

Today we live perilously at or over so many thresholds that we may expect larger and more frequent calamities of all kinds in the future. Insurance is not a real answer, because we all pay the losses in one way or another in the form of higher insurance rates and even more in the damage done to our world. A really major calamity could be too much for the insurance industry. In that event, we would be vividly reminded that insurance is merely a device to spread risks among all the members of a group by creating a pool of funds to pay losses as they occur to various members. When the pool is exhausted, we suffer our own losses ourselves. Many judges and juries need to be reminded of this.

The communications problem is more than one of large company vs. small company. It also increases with the size of the total economy. Every marketing head is supposed to know not only what his customers need, but also what will be the requirements of his customers' customers and even their customers, if he is to predict sales trends and prospects. In a regional economy, this is possible, although difficult. In a national and international economy, it is all but impossible.

Imagine you are a maker of refrigerators. You sell them to

distributors who, in turn, sell them to retailers. When a consumer buys a refrigerator from the retailer's floor, the retailer doesn't reorder from the distributor immediately, unless his stock has already been overdepleted. Nor does the distributor react at once to individual retailer purchases; he waits until his inventory is below minimum to reorder from you, the manufacturer. If there is a general downturn in consumer purchases, the distributor may not know about it for several months until he notices that his retailers are ordering more slowly or in smaller quantities. When your distributors finally do stop buying because their inventory has become too large, it comes as a surprise to you. You have been building inventory in anticipation of continued distributor purchases, but suddenly you also must stop.

At this point, everyone has too much inventory. The retailer has a floorful of unsold refrigerators, the distributor is carrying too much stock, and your warehouse at the factory is full. The full whiplash effect of the slow communication falls on your components suppliers. Yesterday you were pushing them to produce more parts; today you cancel all your orders indefinitely. Since the retailer won't reorder from the distributor until he sells off most of his stock, it will take a long time before the distributor has sold enough to be ready to reorder from you. Certainly you won't start manufacture until your inventory comes down. Therefore, your components suppliers wait even longer. For them, it is truly feast or famine.

What does this tell us? Without even considering the cumulative effect which this chain of circumstances has on the economy as a whole by creating unemployment that in turn reduces consumer purchasing power, it is obvious that the communications system is inadequate to deal with a complex nationwide (and sometimes worldwide) phenomenon. The very scale of the economic system of which you, the refrigerator manufacturer, are a part, has hurt you. Even with the most sophisticated network of business communications and statistical research, the word doesn't get back soon enough to prevent a gentle dip at the consumer level from becoming a catastrophic drop at the manufacturer's level.

One of the virtues of a free enterprise system is that its imbalances are largely self-correcting through the operation of feedbacks from the forces of supply and demand. It is not necessary to understand the whole system, because the economic machine makes its own automatic adjustments. As long as an economy is small or is divided into relatively autonomous subsystems, the feedbacks from imbalances are direct and speedy, so that oscillations in the economy are soon damped and leveled out. But as the economy grows in size and complexity, and subsystems tend to merge into each other, the self-correcting mechanisms become so large and clumsy that they no longer react fast enough to prevent widespread and prolonged disruptions. The economy then tends to run out of control in boom-and-bust cycles.

At this point, when the basic economic laws of supply and demand seem to fail to correct the imbalances promptly, as in 1933, government is called upon to make conscious adjustments to the economy. While economists and politicans may never cease arguing whether these all-wise decisions do more good than harm, we do know that we have yet to experience another 1933 in the United States.

But, in the last few years, new and additional factors are being introduced, making the task even more difficult. Our technological and population growth have added enough direct problems of complexity and crowding. In addition, new environmental problems and the specter of resource scarcity seem to throw all other calculations awry. As the population grows so that the world seems to become smaller, our American economy has become so closely interwoven with those of the rest of the world that we must begin to treat the whole world as a single economy.

All the computer systems in the world can't give the answer. The complexity and scale of our world make it unlikely that they can ever do so. Inanimate objects can be statistically analyzed, provided the appropriate data can be put into the system. But on a world scale, where the unpredictable action of humans rather than the work of a few machines has to be analyzed, this becomes impossible. Today an American wheat farmer needs to know not only how much rain fell on India during the previous monsoon period, but how its and our governments will react to this information if he is to know what and when to plant his crop. He can only guess—and hope he is right. The scale is too big for understanding.

Getting smaller doesn't solve the problem in itself. The antidote to complexity is simplification. Shrinking a business without simplifying it does not reduce the diseconomies of scale. That is one reason why imposing a 10% pay cut in slack times (or establishing a four-day week) can be only a temporary nostrum. Everyone is still on the job doing the same things they did before but, being disgruntled, probably not so well. And there has been no simplification.

Simplification is not easy, however. As E.F. Schumacher says: "Any third-rate engineer or researcher can increase complexity; but it takes a certain flair of real insight to make things simple again."[2] Simplification requires elimination of entire activities, and therefore interferes with vested interests. In government, one never eliminates a department or agency, because that would cost jobs; instead, one creates a new bureau to counteract the first one. Any large organization which has become a bureaucracy tends to react the same way. A new group is formed to put out the fires the first group is lighting.

Overhead breeds overhead. The more people you have in the organization, the more clerks you need to keep track of pay and benefits and provide the perquisites without which big companies can't seem to function. They service the organization itself with the paperwork without which it is tongue-tied. When the organization shrinks, the number of tasks that need to be performed can be shrunk even faster. But they seldom are.

Diseconomies of scale are obvious once we think about them. But usually we don't. Our obsession with growth and the presumed economies of scale have blinded us. An advertising executive talks about a 10% increase in his agency's billing as a laudable achievement. An oil-company vice-president describes the stepped up efforts to produce more oil domestically as necessary and desirable. It is assumed that bigger is better. No one asks why. No one looks beneath the assumption. In our business society, it is still a heresy to question the virtues of growth.

Large size is, of course, necessary in some industries, because the captial investment to make the first unit is now so large. It was not always so. All of our massive industry started on a small scale. Henry Ford began auto manufacture in a garage. The giant capital investment came later as automobile sales volume and technology exploded.

If the diseconomies of scale are so real and so obvious, we may well ask why large companies do not break up into smaller companies, or at least stop growing. Many large companies could be broken up into smaller companies to the benefit of the shareholders, the customers and most of the employees. One powerful group, however, usually opposes any breakups. An economic bureaucracy of any kind, as Richard Goodwin points out, opposes constructive divestitures. To them, any change represents uncertainty "and in the bureaucratic lexicon, uncertainty is a synonym for danger."[3]

Bigness as such is a disadvantage in most corporations. The same thing is true in the economy as a whole. The diseconomies of scale that apply to the corporation are also applicable to the larger entity, although in different ways. Vulnerability to technological damage or collapse is a societal, even more than a corporate, problem.

Our attitude toward our federal government, for instance, has changed over the years as it has multiplied many times in size. Forty years ago, when the federal government was relatively small, the people in federal (and in state) jobs seemed to be of higher quality than those appointed to local positions. People tended to look to the federal government because it was better run. The proliferation of agencies and functions came later. Now, even the liberals who want government to do everything, recognize that it has become a morass of incompetence. Today, despite perennial corruption, local governments seem to be able to handle local problems better than national or state bureaucracies, because they have to be responsive to local needs and demands and are closer to them.

The quality and effectiveness of communications is crucial to the operation of all organizations, formal or informal. Management of a business or of a government becomes more difficult as size increases, despite the aid of the best in modern technology.

The scale problem of the world as a whole must concern us most of all, because it combines the sum of all the individual diseconomies with the overwhelming problem of population. The more people there are, the less well any system works.

All of the technological skills which we use to keep the world from falling apart at its present population level would provide us a wonderfully better world if there were not so many of us. As long as population grows, it is a race that we can only lose.

Today we run faster and faster to stay in the same place. Despite the increased material wealth of the last thirty years, we seem to be no better off. The increasing scale of our enterprises and the growing complexity of our interrelationships make life increasingly difficult. It has taken all the miracles of new technology to keep us abreast of our problems. Because technology has not fulfilled all its promise, we blame it for our failures. We would do better to blame ourselves and our numbers.

4

Who Is the Company Run For?

THE GROWTH OF OUR ECONOMIC SYSTEM received great impetus from the invention of the limited liability corporation. Because of its inherent advantages as a form of organization, the corporation began to dominate industrial life. It proved to be the vehicle by which capitalism could achieve its greatest potential.

Infinitely expandable, flexible enough to adjust to a wide range of opportunities, the corporate form has evolved as a master matrix. In the course of its evolution, however, it has changed beyond recognition from the original concept of enabling a few people to cast their lot together to build a business enterprise, usually of limited size and scope.

The basic legal structure of the corporation has changed little from its early form. If its inventors studied the modern publicly held corporation, however, they would find its actual operation today almost unrecognizable.

The equity in a corporation is still owned by its shareholders.

Who Is the Company Run For?

Other groups have claims on the company of one kind or another, but they are not owners. Customers are entitled to a safe and honest product. The creditors have a right to be paid. The banks and noteholders are entitled to their interest on the debt and to the principal when due. The Federal government gets its share of the profits through the corporate income tax. State and local governments and the community itself have their claims and rights. The employees are due their pay when earned, their pensions as accrued and when vested and are entitled to a safe working environment, plus a host of other claims on the company.

Stockholders elect directors who, in turn, elect officers. The officers run the company, presumably on behalf of the shareholders who, indirectly, put them there. But do they really? In fact, they rarely do, unless the goals of the shareholders happen to coincide with those of the management.

First, managers now have responsibilities beyond those to shareholders. Originally, corporations were supposed to be run solely for the benefit of the shareholders. Modern views have considerably modified this. It is now popular to affirm that the company is run not just for the shareholders, but to some extent for the employees, too. The community as a whole as well as government, local, state, and federal, have a stake in each enterprise. Customers and suppliers also have an interest. Managers understand and react to the pressures to meet these responsibilities to the extent necessary.

Perhaps recent social theory has now recognized what the shareholder had forgotten—that all along the enterprise had responsibilities in other areas, as every citizen does. Shareholders are now allowing the company to assume these responsibilities.

But even before these new responsibilities were considered, the shareholder, who is the titular owner, was the truly forgotten man. In practice, shareholders have very little to say about how corporations are run, except in small companies in which a very few people own or control the majority of the stock.

In the modern giant corporation, the directors look for leadership more to the managers than to the shareholders. They are dependent upon management for their directors' fees, their perquisites, the information about the company available to them, and their very jobs. It is management who determines who the officers and directors shall be. Unless the shareholders revolt, which they rarely do so long as the company is doing reasonably well, management is entirely self-perpetuating.

Richard Goodwin has stressed that

> Whenever widely dispersed property comes under central management, the result is bureaucracy. In a bureaucracy the managers are also owners, at least to the extent of their power to determine value. That is among the reasons that bureaucratic structures always have some interests distinct from those of its constituencies.[1]

Most companies are really run for the benefit of the managers, with such obeisances to other groups as protection of the managers' own interests requires. This is not a cynical view, but is a fact which most managers will admit when their public relations guard is down.

Quoting Richard Goodwin again:

> The executive is able to command excess compensation even though he is a mere "employee" because the corporation is

unowned. He is only accountable to other employees; most of those who are in a position to object have their own interest in maintaining high levels of compensation, and only large rewards will attract desired talent to the uncertain, career-long struggle for position. . . .

Management skills, even at the higher levels, are not awesomely complex, technical or difficult. The necessary natural endowment is far more widely distributed than the talent to be a robber baron, a nuclear physicist or a successful magazine editor. The value of management talent is thus less intrinsic, less based upon a personal capacity to create, seize or command a segment of the wealth-producing apparatus, and more dependent upon its suitability, its correspondence, to the functional needs of established enterprise. And the other face of managerial skill, the capacity to rise within the bureaucracy, acquires its value, almost by definition, from the existence of the organization.[2]

Knowing this, one better understands managers' obsession with growth. Whether the earnings per share improve or not, managers of a growing company command higher salaries, acquire more and fancier perquisites, and gain more power as the company grows. They are held in high esteem because of their obvious success, even in cases where the increase in profits for umpteen consecutive years has not kept up with the rate of inflation. In such cases, the common stock of their companies may be gradually sliding backwards in terms of value in real dollars, but, so long as the nominal price per share climbs, they are deemed to be successful. It is not difficult for managers to maintain working control indefinitely.

Shareholders seldom realize that management's interests

may at times be precisely contrary to their own. I remember one corporate candidate for turnaround acquisition which we spent many months seeking to acquire, eventually in vain. It was a substantial company, the stock of which was traded on the American Stock Exchange, but it was no longer making money. It had two operating divisions. The older and smaller division made a consistently profitable proprietary line of machinery used in automobile manufacture. The newer and larger division did highly skilled job shop machining for the airplane industry and, although that division had once been profitable, it was then (1959) losing money at an increasing rate. Our analysis indicated that there was no future in the highly competitive aircraft machining business, so the larger division should be closed and the company should be shrunk to the small proprietary business which always made money.

Since we could not afford to buy the company for cash, we sought a merger with our company. We hoped that the company's owners would recognize that this was their shareholders' best hope and that we were the people to do the job. Negotiations continued for months. They started to bog down, however, when their president, who dominated the board, confessed that he could not see disposing of the loss operation since that would mean moving his executive offices to the smaller plant, which he felt would not be suitable for a company with several thousand shareholders. Personal image was more important to this manager than corporate success. The company later found a more tractable buyer, and the operation finally sank with all colors flying.

The difference of view between the managers and the stockholders of a corporation is particularly apparent when a divestiture is necessary. Irving Kristol gives a case in point:

. . . one major corporation seems to be having considerable difficulty in divesting itself of a large and profitable subsidiary, as required by the Federal Trade Commission . . . there is an easy way out for the company, one which the FTC could not possibly object to—spinning off the subsidiary to the company's shareholders. The company has rejected this possibility on the grounds that it is not in the ''best interests'' of these shareholders.

But why isn't it? It is hard to see why, and I rather imagine that if those shareholders were given the chance to vote on the issue, they might well decide that a spin-off is decidedly in their best interests. They will not, of course, be given any such opportunity. For it is obvious that life would be more interesting—and presumably in the end more profitable—for the company's executives if *they* had 800 million dollars or so to play with, rather than seeing all the money vanish into the pockets of its stockholders. . . . the executives do not even seem to realize that they are involved in a situation that suggests a potential conflict of interests, and that there is an ethical aspect to their decision to which attention should be paid.[3]

Managers are human. The power, prestige and financial rewards that come with success are intensely satisfying. From their personal point of view, they take pride in making the company bigger. They gain credit with the shareholders, too, even though the shareholders might well do better if the company had not grown. No one can forget the magic names of IBM, Polaroid, and Xerox, and the tremendous growth they achieved, to the great benefit of their shareholders. ''Let's do it again!''

Big firms tend to be political entities. Managers would have difficulty cutting them back to a smaller, more profitable, level even if they wanted to because:

1　If they tried, the stockholders would think (wrongly) that the managers are insane and would probably fire them before they could show results; and
2　Severe shrinking would produce so much unemployment that the managers would have the government and the community on their backs.

For personal reasons, most managers would not want to make the company smaller anyway because:

1　Regardless of high profits, people equate high salaries with high volume, so that they would probably be paid less or at least no more.
2　They would lose prestige by running a smaller company.
3　They would be mavericks. Few people want to be "different," particularly once they have spent their lives working their way to corporate high command by doing the right things and avoiding errors.
4　They believe that eliminating redundant staff would irrevocably damage the interpersonal relations with their associates. (After all, skill in interpersonal relations is a major key to personal success in large organizations.)
5　Finally, they would consider shrinking an admission of failure.

I know of one substantial conglomerate that ingested dozens of companies in the late sixties but now finds that many of them are sick. The top man cannot yet face admitting error by dumping these bad acquisitions for less than book value, which would appear as a big corporate loss, even though surgery is the only remedy. Unless he can change his mind or be booted out, the total company may be brought down because of his unwillingness to admit error. Pride is a valuable attribute when things go well; but when they don't, it can be a fatal weakness.

When the company is growing, everyone feels fine. The management job is much easier. You promote your best people and still have room for all the rest, even those you know you would be better off without. When you are growing, you don't have to fire anybody. If they are not doing their share, you can just stop promoting them and the company grows past them. Management mistakes can be buried and forgotten. What a lovely solution!

The manager of the large company, like the politician, need not be really interested in long-range corporate results. Among the five hundred largest industrial corporations, there are few in which the chief executive officer can expect to be in office more than eight to ten years. Many can expect tenures of five years or less. Until they reach the corporate summit, their attention is unlikely to have been directed toward the overall welfare of the corporation, but instead to the immediate problems of their particular area of responsibility. Like politicians, they have every reason to be shortsighted. A single top man, unless, like Harold Geneen of ITT, he has an unusually long time in command, rarely has enough effect on the company to become apparent while he is still in office. Usually he is long retired before the programs he set in motion, for better or worse, come to fruition.

The compulsion to act is one of the most unreliable engines of growth. "Don't just stand there. Do something!" If your research and marketing departments have completed their studies on the new superfandango, there are compelling reasons to put it into production as soon as possible. What will your people do if they aren't pushing ahead on new projects? If they don't have enough work to do, you don't need them. They know it, so they usually keep up the level of activity, whether anything is accomplished or not.

Some people are unable to make the transition from worker to manager because they can't stand not doing something every minute. A manager is supposed to plan and direct the work of others, not do it himself. Once a military battle has been joined, a general who has made all possible preparations and set the forces in motion has little to do but worry and wait. Many managers cannot stand having an idle moment. They are always working hard, always overburdened and always in the fray, even though they are presumably paid to stay out of it.

Businessmen are so used to working frenetically that they are ill at ease when one job is finished and they don't know what to plunge into next. The businessman may know that theoretically the manager who has little to do is running a good show, but in his gut he doesn't believe it. Even if he is his own boss, he is so imbued with the work ethic that he is nervous when things go too smoothly. For him, security is being so busy that he doesn't have time to think.

Many an acquisition is made not to increase the profit per share of the acquiring company, but to provide management with a new world to conquer. A manager knows himself well when he can tell the difference between the avowed reason (improving the share profits) and the real reason (enhancing his own image with himself and others), even if he never admits it. When he works for others he has an added reason to be insecure.

If he doesn't act busy, his boss may think he lacks drive and initiative.

Because of this, the shareholder gets the same kind of government of the company that the citizen gets from the representatives he elects to political office. The manager, like the politician, is so susceptible to the lobbying efforts of groups or individuals who have special axes to grind that he overlooks the general interests of his real constituency. The owners of the company, unless they sell their stock or sell the company as a whole, will still be deeply affected by how the company is doing ten, twenty, or more years from now, but the manager will be long gone. He cannot have the same concern.

Because a large company, like a large ship, cannot easily or quickly be set on a new course, it must plan well ahead. But, since the manager will often be retired before the change is completed, these plans tend to be little more than elaborate extrapolations of the past. The answers tend to be assumed because the real questions are seldom asked.

Even though the large company can attract the finest business brains by rewarding them handsomely, it fails to encourage more than superficial attention to basic long term problems of our economy as a whole. In the long pull (and that is what the stockholder is interested in), the prospects of the nation's and world's total economy are of fundamental importance to every business. One cannot assume, as most managers do now, that the climate in which they will operate will change little if at all in the years to come.

If the shareholders have little or no influence over management, managers will tend to make decisions without taking shareholder interests into account. They are not opposed to the shareholders and their interest, just neutral to them. In the same way, politicians are generally indifferent to the general interests of their constituents, except to the extent that they represent effective ballot power. They are not evil in this attitude, merely human.

Why does anyone become a shareholder? Assuming that too little stock is purchased to entitle the buyer to a significant voice in the company's management, there are only two reasons to buy: 1) high dividend income from the stock, either present or prospective, and 2) the hope of a substantial increase in the stock value so that a subsequent sale can be made for a capital gain. Since, in today's economic climate, high income can be obtained from other relatively safe forms of investment, the desire for capital gain is usually the compelling reason to buy. We hope that the value of the stock will rise more than enough to offset the effects of the expected inflation.

Capital gain has a special advantage under Federal income tax laws because it is taxed at lower rates than ordinary income. Years ago, capital gains tax rates were set at about half of regular income tax rates, partly to encourage capital investment in a growth economy. Another reason was that long term gains were not considered really to be income, since a profitable sale is one-time recognition of an increase in value that may have been spread over years of gradual appreciation. In more recent years, much apparent capital gain really represents inflation and, to that extent, does not reflect increase in real value of the security.

Although the individual investor may buy stocks in the hope of capital gains, in the long run the basic value of a stock can only be a reflection of the dividend yield in effect or reasonably in prospect. Companies that pay no cash dividends or only tiny percentages of their earnings command good prices only when it is believed that earnings will climb in the future so that the eventual dividend yield on today's cost price will be high.

The New York Stock Exchange, in its TV commercials, suggests that you invest in stocks so that you can grow with America. Much of the expectation of growth in specific equity values depends on the belief that all equities will benefit from growth in population, growth in resource consumption, and growth in energy use. If this hope were greatly diminished, and we recognized that the *average* company can expect to sell about the same number of units in the future as in the past it would be apparent that only a few companies could grow. The successful investor would be the one who picked out those companies that would do better than the average and avoided the equal number that would do worse. Investing thus is a far more demanding task than during those halcyon days when anyone could be an investment expert by picking stocks at random.

If one is not skilled enough to identify in advance the companies which are going to buck the percentages by growing, one is better off to invest in a stable company that is not expansion-minded and, therefore, does not need to plow back all its earnings into financing its growth. Such a company, after it has accumulated adequate cash reserves, can afford to pay out 100% of its earnings as dividends.

But, under present conditions, this is not practical. The combination of the corporate income tax on company earnings and the individual income tax on all dividends received by the shareholders effectively deters payment of dividends. The present law is not only inequitable double taxation, it is bad tax policy—and the latter is more serious. The existence of this form of double taxation, together with the provision for lower rates on capital gains, clearly stimulates growth for growth's sake.

Because the tax rate on capital gains is about half the rate on dividend income, wealthier shareholders (in higher tax brackets) generally prefer that dividends be modest in amount, so that the company will become more valuable by plowing back its earnings into its operations. In this way, the value of the stock will presumably climb and the shareholder will eventually be able to cash in by selling the stock for a capital gain, taxed at a lower rate than the dividends he might otherwise have received.

If capital gains tax rates were the same as ordinary income tax rates, there would be far less incentive to avoid ordinary income tax consequences by retaining the funds in the corporation. If there were no advantageous capital gains tax rate, it is even possible to imagine a company involved in a dying business paying out more than 100% of profits in dividends, thus affecting a gradual liquidation, without adverse tax consequences.

Eliminating the tax benefits for capital gains would automatically reduce the emphasis on growth in company operation *per se*. Today's emphasis on earnings would be replaced by a deep concern with dividend yield.

Management is reluctant to pay out dividends, because they reduce the funds it has at its disposal. Today, managers have a wonderful rationale for being stingy in dividend payments: they must save company funds for needed expansion. Growth is the perfect reason for management hoarding, and has been so effective that most managements now believe it. If growth becomes a dirty word, one wonders what new excuse for not paying dividends will be invented.

Two changes in the Federal income tax laws would correct

this problem. The first would be to eliminate the special tax rate on capital gains and treat them as ordinary income.[4] Today, a large proportion of capital gains represents inflation. Therefore, provision should be made for reducing the amount of the capital gain subject to tax by the extent of the inflation during the period held. Congressional consideration of reducing capital gains rates in some ratio to the length of time the security has been held is another way of reaching the same end.

Second, and more important, I propose that all dividends paid should be deducted from taxable corporate income. The corporate tax rate could be set at the level that would protect the treasury against loss of revenue from the sum of the present two taxes (corporate income tax and individual income tax) on corporate earnings. If the corporation paid no dividends, it would pay tax on all its earnings; if it distributed a large proportion of its earnings, its tax would be greatly reduced, but the individual taxpayer who received the dividend would pay income tax at his applicable income tax rate, depending upon his personal income bracket.

Income tax systems which provide that the corporation pays a high tax on all its income but passes on dividends to its shareholders substantially tax free have been tried. Such systems have the effect of benefiting primarily those in high tax brackets by reducing their income, otherwise subject to tax at the top rate. My suggested plan has no such effect; each shareholder pays tax in his income tax bracket on the dividends received.

One may object that the IRS will not do so well as at present, because the average bracket of the individual taxpayer will be less than the 48% rate most corporations now pay. There are answers to this:

Who Is the Company Run For?

1   Although the corporate income tax rate for income over $25,000 a year is generally 48%, because of various offsets and credits and the effect of a lower rate for corporations with less than $25,000 income, the average effective corporate income rate is only 38%.

2   Inflation has raised the income of the average taxpayer into higher brackets in the last few years. I suggest that studies would show that the average shareholder (whose income would be expected to be higher than that of the average taxpayer) would be in a bracket near 38%, particularly if it is remembered that the shareholders with the large holdings in companies are generally in the highest brackets.

3   The extra dividends resulting from the encouragement of the dividend credit would be paid out instead of keeping the money in the company. Under present law, the individual shareholder, when he eventually sells, pays tax on such earnings to the extent that they increased the value of his stock, but only at capital gains tax rates instead of ordinary income tax rates. (Under present laws, if the shareholder still owns the stock at death, there is no capital gains tax.)

4   Most of the money paid out in dividends, if retained by the company instead, would be spent either in capital investments tax-deductible over a period of years or for current expenses tax-deductible immediately, thus reducing future corporate tax payments.

5   Finally, to the extent that the treasury might suffer a loss in total revenue despite the above offsets (and I really doubt that it would), the corporate income tax rates could be increased above the 48% level, even as

high as 60%. I would not rule out consideration of some kind of progressive corporate income tax, as it would also act as a deterrent to unnecessary growth or bigness.

In essence, the present lower tax rate on capital gains no longer really benefits the shareholder. Instead, it encourages the company to plow back its earnings into new and larger projects, so that any tangible rewards to the shareholder are deferred to a very indefinite future. Corporate growth should no longer be encouraged by tax policy.

A corporate income tax allowing full credit against taxable income for all dividends paid would encourage the distribution to shareholders of much if not all of the earnings, unless it is clear that the company (rather than just the managers) will benefit from retaining some of the earnings to invest in ongoing projects. If management failed to pay substantial dividends, but retained much of the earnings for reinvestment in company growth, the owners would scream loudly unless they were convinced that the purposes for which the money was retained justified the high corporate income tax that could be avoided by dividend distribution. Once they compared the discounted value to them of a future sale of the appreciated stock with the present value of a cash dividend, it would take a lot of convincing. The practical effect of such a tax would be to place in the hands of the shareholders a short leash with which to restrain managerial exuberance.

Present tax laws encourage even the controlling shareholders in small companies to plow earnings back into new corporate projects and investments in order to avoid or postpone the tax on that income if distributed to them as dividends. If full corporate income tax were paid only on earnings retained in the business and not distributed as dividends, any new program would receive as much critical analysis as if the shareholder were making his initial investment in the company.

One hears the argument today that the general anti-business attitude in the United States (and worldwide) has so hamstrung business development that we are not getting the capital investment that is desperately needed to develop our economy and improve our productivity. Unquestionably, if corporations did not retain the greater part of earnings for reinvestment, the cries would be even louder. If, however, most of corporate earnings were paid out as dividends, shareholders would be provided far greater funds to reinvest (even after income tax which, in total, would have no greater impact than today). Their decisions would not be made for them automatically by managers who keep the funds in the business, often for purposes of their own. Investors, as a group, would be more likely to be concerned that what they are investing in has some basic merit and is not merely a gimmick to make the company bigger.

It is unquestionably true that new equity capital is hard for a business to obtain without major dilution of the shares of existing equity owners. Such dilution is often unacceptable, so most businesses have resorted to debt, often short term, to get the funds they deem necessary for their operations. The stock market downswing of the early 1970s aggravated an already tight situation by wiping out a mountain of paper value of securities which could otherwise have supported increasing debt loads, so that it is now more difficult than ever to obtain new capital on acceptable terms.

In the short run, we can only infer why stock prices rise or fall. Buyers and sellers usually don't advertise their reasons;

they just act. People on Wall Street can make shrewd guessses as to why investors are enthusiastic one day and panicky the next, but they have no real clue as to what the real motivations are. In the long run, evaluation of basic economic trends is decisive.

The stock market reflects the combined foresight of a host of people. I suspect that some of these people are concerned about something that the chartists and other investment industry economists have never thought about: where the world is going. Business economists have tended to be so concerned with extrapolating past trends that they have never asked whether the rules might be changing, perhaps irrevocably. No wonder they were caught unawares by the market drop of the early seventies.

It would seem that, from now on, the shareholder is best served by the managers who make maximum use of the initial financial resources provided to them, rather than those who use all the shareholder's profits to invest in new projects unanticipated when the original investment was made. Much of present rhetoric in favor of the need for major investments is self-serving, not in the interest of the shareholder, and probably not in that of the economy as a whole.

In this instance, shareholder interest and long-range public interest are parallel. Just as the shareholder can scarcely expect the manager to think of him first, the citizen has the same concern about his political representative. The citizen has to be vigilant to be sure that the political representative truly represents all his constituents and not just those influential few who may really determine his political future.

What can the individual shareholder do? Not much, except in his choice of companies in which to invest. In making this selection, it is helpful to know where the power is.

Who Is the Company Run For?

The officers and directors of most large corporations, as a group, hold less than 3% of the outstanding stock. Yet once they obtain control of the corporation, barring catastrophe, they have it forever. That doesn't mean that they are bad men. On the contrary, most are conscientious, hard working, and capable, but their vision is often sharply limited. In intelligence and ability business leaders are at the top of our society, but they tend to live in their own narrow world. They communicate largely with each other or with those who serve them, either inside or outside their organizations. Nowhere is this more obvious than in the myopia of the automotive hierarchy in and about Detroit.

Proposals to break the tight grip of management by greater minority-shareholder representation on the board of directors have had little impact. Applauding corporate leaders for showing corporate social responsibility is desirable, but does not get at the root of the problem. Mindless growth is the problem. So long as management can plow back most of corporate earnings into new projects, whether they make long range sense or not, it matters little whether the company has good affirmative-action programs on minority employment or supports educational televison.

It is important, however, who are elected directors. If you want to know about a company, look at the composition of the board of directors. Is it an "inside" or a predominantly "outside" board? (In looking at directors' affiliations in the annual report, count major customers, suppliers, lawyers, investment bankers, and bankers as "insiders.")

Managers who are sincerely interested in the best for their company can benefit greatly from an independent, predominantly outside board of directors. I have been on both sides of the fence in different companies with mixed inside and outside boards. In general, I believe the best boards are those composed of one or two members of management, with all the rest outsiders.

When there are a number of inside members, board meetings tend to become operating meetings, which they should not be, instead of policy meetings, which they should. When there are several insiders on the board, they usually report to and work for one of their number (the chief executive officer). This can inhibit their open participation in policy matters.

Even in the case of the preferred outside board one insider is more than a match for a whole board of outsiders, no matter how able and distinguished they may be, because:

1　The insider works fulltime on the company's affairs; they do not.

2　The insider controls all the channels of information about corporate affairs, while they must learn much of what they know from him (or, at least, through him).

3　The insider not only controls the destinies of individual employees of the company but directors serve as such largely at his sufferance (even when he hasn't picked them himself), because few of them control enough stock to vote themselves on. He even determines their compensation.

Assuming that you are an outside director and that the board meetings don't degenerate into operating meetings, what can you really do? It has been said that the only function of a board is to decide, at each meeting, whether to fire or keep the president. This is an over-simplification of the theory that authority and responsibility should be fully delegated to the administrator and the board should stay out of his way as long as the results are satisfactory. There is some truth in this, but not all the truth.

Directors have a very real responsibility not so much to tell the administration what to do as to be sure that it is doing a competent and honest job. More than that, they have the responsibility to give the administration the benefit of their knowledge and insights about business operation in general, particularly in their fields of special skill.

A good director need not (in fact, should not) get into the details of how the company's products are made. It is the questions he asks that are important. What is the company particularly good at? What are the corporate goals? How does our company fit into its industry and the economy in general? What are the marketing channels? How meaningful are our financial statements? Are they well organized and timely and do they give the information needed for sound policy decisions? How good are our cost figures? Who decides product pricing and how does it compare with competition, keeping quality and service in mind? And a thousand other questions. In brief, he looks at the whole forest; management is more often concerned with individual trees.

Most large and many smaller corporations have organized corporate audit committees composed entirely of outside directors who meet at least annually with the company auditors without the presence of management. It is the job of that committee to look for weaknesses in control, conflicts of interest within management, and any kind of monkey business which the auditors might have a chance to uncover. Since the auditors are selected by the management (although usually subject to perfunctory board and even shareholder approval), the committee must watch to be sure the auditor-management relationship is not too cozy. Although corporate fraud can be concealed even from the most thorough auditors, it is more dificult to hide a massive fraud (such as the Equity Funding case)[5] when a conscientious outside audit committee asks the right questions.

Even in a small company wholly owned and operated by a single person or family, the owners can benefit enormously by having several outside directors who are not beholden to management or the owners. They should receive a monthly stipend for their services (paying by the meeting implies that their only value is their bodily presence). It is worth having outsiders just for the stimulation of their quarterly look at the total company as it relates to the economy as a whole, rather than in relation only to the particular fire to be extinguished at the moment.

In the long run it is better not to have your lawyer, your banker or your investment advisor as a director. They can serve you best in their special capacities without being on the board. You need generalists, not specialists.

Brilliant businessmen who run their own corporations are often a disappointment as directors of other companies, because they are so involved in their own corporate problems that they have inadequate time to do the necessary homework. They may study all the material the chairman provides them and they may attend all the meetings, but they seldom are used to the kind of leisurely consideration of the total economic picture that is helpful in making major policy decisions. They need a minimum of briefing, however, and can be helpful on specific problems almost immediately.

If we eliminate lawyers, bankers, investment advisors, and many top businessmen as candidates for directors, who is left?

Picking a director is an important decision, particularly since, once he is elected, it is very embarrassing to fail to reelect him annually if he doesn't perform as well as you had hoped. Some years ago, as CEO, I had a rare free choice in picking a person to fill a board vacancy. I spent several months pondering it and finally invited a businessman who was particularly strong in marketing, where we were weak. He was a good choice, but it is not always so. Choosing a director can be risky, but so is running blind.

We are seeing more professional directors today. One may ask what does a college president or a clergyman or biophysicist or even a blue-collar worker know about running a corporation? The answer is that they don't have to know how to run it, but that they may be able to sense some of the latent forces that will deeply influence the corporate prospects in the future. The business community has been too inbred and it can only benefit by broadening its membership to include other sectors of our society.

Directors, of course, are expected to represent the shareholders. Good ones do so partly by constantly reminding management for whom it is working and partly by making management look at the premises behind their assumptions that bigger is always better and that there is only one direction to go. We need more truly independent and able directors.

Active shareholders, aided by the courts, are beginning to loosen ever-so-slightly management's grip on big, publicly owned corporations. Anti-discrimination legislation has stimulated a very few companies to take on women or blacks as directors. In an unprecedented move, a Federal court has forced the restructuring of Northrop Aviation Corporation by adding enough outside directors to take control away from the insiders (*Business Week*, February 24, 1975). A gradual trend may be seen toward reducing management's self-perpetuating control of the corporation.

I am well aware what a nuisance it is to have to bring into the corporate family people who may not seem to be very helpful. In the first place, they don't understand the language. We feel as if we were explaining the subtleties of professional football to a Tibetan monk. Even worse, many of these new directors don't trust us and don't agree with our goals or methods. We may feel that some are virtually uneducable by our terms. Some of them are.

But we can survive misunderstanding and mistrust if we learn from them. We businessmen are the ones who need educating. I believe that broadening shareholder representation on corporate boards is absolutely necessary, if only as a sort of insurance policy against our going off in a totally wrong direction without even being aware of it. Maybe we won't cover as much ground in board meetings on operating matters, such as this year's capital budget and sales projections, but we may well gain some new insights about what we are and where we really should want to go.

Yet a more effective board of directors can do nothing about some basic aspects of corporate economics. The relationship between the shareholder and the corporation under our present laws inhibits any fundamental change in the corporate power structure. If we become aware of how it works, maybe we can remedy that.

Until the basic tax laws are changed, however, the company will be run for the benefit of the managers. It is unfortunate that, in their hot pursuit of their version of corporate success, the purpose of doing business at all is often forgotten. If not for the continuing need to raise additional capital on attractive terms to finance new growth, the external pressures to improve Return on Investment (ROI) and Earnings per Share (EPS) would diminish.

Certainly, shareholders today enjoy seeing the stock go up in price. It is a game for them, too, but it is a game special to this generation of stock market watchers. If you don't get much in the way of dividends, you have to have something to hope for. But capital gain is a substitute for dividend return, which should be the most important long-run measure of corporate success.

In big business, the vast amorphous group of shareholders are too passive and too remote to have any influence on corporate affairs. Despite the new pressures of minority shareholders for a voice in management, they have received only lip service. The corporate statutes of each state, basically unchanged since early in the century, give them little foothold.

Since the stockholder can rarely have any influence on corporate affairs, his only recourse is to sell his stock if he doesn't agree with management decisions. In the large publicly owned company, he can usually turn his investment into cash on short notice.

In the long run, the best opportunities for gain are in the smaller businesses, but you are locked into the investment, often for a lifetime or even more. Each investor must weigh the value of potential gain against the need for liquidity, before buying a stock. The smaller company has limited access to the capital market, because it cannot offer liquidity. This is a major handicap of smallness. The securities laws of the last forty years have aggravated this situation by complex regulations that only big business can afford to cope with but which provide little practical protection to the individual investor.

Who Is the Company Run For?

Should the tax laws be changed as I have proposed to encourage payment of a higher percentage of profits in dividends, the stockholder would have a significant kind of cash gain even in a small closely held company. The liquidity of the public market would be less important to him, because he would hold the stock for substantial income rather than until a good time to sell. Small companies would thus be better able to compete with the industrial giants for equity money.

There would be no tax barrier to liquidating a company, once its original purpose had been accomplished. If we reach a world in which employment is not relied on as the principal means of distributing income, the employees would not suffer if corporate life ended; their lives would not depend on it. Nor need the managers suffer; they can boast that they brought their ship to port. A corporation need not live forever.

If we are to survive and thrive in the perilous world that lies ahead, we need relief from dinosaurism and a return to the kind of adaptability that gave our mammalian ancestors their first start in a giant reptilian world.

5

What is "Job Philosophy"?

WHEN THE CAVEMAN WENT HUNTING, his concern was to come back with the meat and skins to provide food and clothing for himself and his family. When the head of the modern household brings home the bacon, he or she performs the same function, but the reward is usually a paycheck which can be translated into food and clothing for the whole family. The paycheck is the representation of the work presumed to have been done, entitling the employee to be supported by that segment of society represented by his employer.

In our large, interdependent and highly specialized society the financial reward often becomes the sole motivation, because we do not see the effects of our work on the society as a whole nor often even on the particular organization as a whole. We can hardly expect a bus driver in a large city to consider philosophically his role in keeping the economy moving. It will not occur to him (and even if it does, he may not care) that stopping to pick up a particular rider when the bus is already behind schedule may enable that person to get to his place of work in

94

time to perform a vital job that otherwise would not be done. We have all heard: "For want of a nail, the shoe was lost . . ." but we rarely act as if it were really true, because our economic system is so complex that tracing the effects of our actions or inactions through the economy is impossibly complicated.

In a small self-contained community, the interaction of cause and effect is more obvious. Each person's role in keeping the economy going is understood. If he fails to do his job, others will let him know about it promptly. If the shoemaker neglects his work, the community will go unshod; he will be subjected to powerful pressure to get busy. But in a large economy, no single person's work or failure makes a significant mark.

Likewise, in a small or middle-sized business organization, the corporate purposes are usually well understood. Each worker knows that certain results are expected if a wage is to be earned. In the large corporate organization, however, and particularly in big government, the overall purpose is too remote to influence the actions of the individual deep in the hierarchy. His main incentive is to protect his job by opting for inaction—a safer course than trying to make a maximum personal contribution toward advancing the purposes of the total organization.

In a large, crowded world, there is a natural tendency to forget that the work done should contribute to the strength of the economy as a whole, not merely provide pay for the individual worker, which may be spent in the community for personal purposes. People tend to disregard what is being accomplished by the performance of their jobs, being concerned only with the wages and salaries the employees receive and their effects upon the community in which they are spent. This is "job philosophy": the attitude that the employment itself is more important than whether anything of value is produced by those employed.

What are typical examples of concentrating one's attention on jobs only for the sake of having them, instead of concern with what is accomplished? Featherbedding is perhaps the most obvious: insisting on two people doing and getting paid for what one person can easily do (this creates nothing additional that can be defined as wealth.)

Since union organizations are essentially interested in income for their members, it may be expected that they will have little direct concern for what is produced. It is remarkable, however, that most unions have not resisted automation which eliminated jobs. Instead, their leaders came to believe that automation was necessary to meet competition. They accepted the argument that better production would create as many new jobs as it wiped out, by enlarging the market as it made possible a lower priced or new or better product. Some unions, on the other hand, did maintain their resistance to change. The building trades, for example, have consistently opposed improvements in construction methods which might weaken their tight control over the jobs the industry provides.

Featherbedding has eaten up all possible technological gains in productivity in some industries. The Florida East Coast Railway provides clear before-and-after evidence. The railroad, which runs 348 miles from Jacksonville to Miami, was hit by a bitter strike in January, 1963. The owners decided to continue operations anyway with new help. They took the opportunity to eliminate all featherbedding rules at all levels and to apply the best precepts of business management to make the railroad truly efficient. Despite violent union resistance, the railroad not only continued in operation but began to make money. "In 1954, 4000 FEC employees handled 1.2 billion ton miles of freight. In 1973, approximately 1000 employees handled almost 2 billion ton miles more efficiently, more safely and with better service" (*Business Week*, September 7, 1974, p. 66). Productivity was multiplied more than six times.

Although railroads probably have more featherbedding than most other industries, this increase in productivity through its elimination shows clearly how job philosophy has dragged us down—wherever it appears. Waste of people is not only union-generated. Featherbedding exists at all levels of operation, not excluding the executive suite. All of us pay for it in higher prices for everything we buy.

In 1974, when the production workers went on strike at the U.S. Borax & Chemical Corporation operation at Boron, California, 450 white collar employees went to work to keep a plant going which normally employed 1,400, largely union members. In a few months, the untrained scabs were setting production records. The results spotlighted past inefficiencies, involving a long and gradual deterioration in labor relations during which management had permitted gross overmanning and featherbedding in order to keep temporary labor peace (*Fortune* magazine, December, 1974).

The same thing happens to most of us when we don't have enough to do to keep us occupied. Efficiency suffers when there are more people to do the job than needed. I remember, during World War II, being one of a group of five naval officers who ran a radio station combined with a ciphering and deciphering facility on a round-the-clock basis. Our commander asked Washington for more help, because we were almost swamped with work. He hoped to get two more officers and would have been glad to get one. The Naval Bureau of Personnel sent us eight additional officers all at one time. Unfortunately, we had too much of a good thing. The station was never so efficient again.

Unions are not the only groups to promote job philosophy. Any profession which restricts entry to its ranks is likely to have monopolistic leanings, deliberate or not. Because medical training is both long and expensive and medical schools have room for only the most promising students, there is an acute scarcity of doctors. As a result, individual doctors tend to have more work than they can handle and are able to concentrate their efforts in the most financially rewarding directions. Despite an obvious need, the use of paramedics and nurses to handle many of the doctors' necessary tasks has been resisted by the medical profession. Although the fear of lowering professional standards is the apparent good argument, the real reasons may be more economic than professional.

Nor does the legal profession come off clean. Since most laws are written and enacted largely by lawyers, their plea that the increasing complexities of new legislation require more frequent calls on their services is self-serving. Meanwhile, bar associations continue to be more concerned about inroads on the profession by accountants, realtors, and others than by the derelictions of their own members.

It is job philosophy when any community uses legislative influence to prevent the closing of an obsolete governmental installation, because it does not want to lose the flow of funds into the local economy. Every group urging a high tariff to prevent foreign competition with American industry is asking all consumers to pay higher prices in order to keep certain

What Is "Job Philosophy"?

Americans fully employed. (Even more important than that: our long term selfish national interest should demand that, rather than use part of our limited supply of nonrenewable natural resources we encourage other countries to use theirs by allowing their goods to be imported and marketed here.)

Every company which puts out products with quick obsolescence is asking the economy to carry an extra burden. Every government department which is more concerned with providing jobs to placeholders than performing a creative function is an added albatross around our collective neck.

Job philosophy is found in many guises and disguises. A Washington news item (October 2, 1974) reported that "American women are deciding not to have babies at such an increasing rate—3 million as of now—that last year's fertility low may be surpassed, the Census Bureau reported Tuesday. 'That's both good and bad,' said a spokesman. 'Short-term benefits will be relief from economic pressures. Long-term problems could be unemployed teachers and a housing slump,' said the Bureau." That Census Bureau spokesman is talking job philosophy. If teachers are unemployed and houses are not built because they are not needed as the population to be served is smaller, why should the country persist in wanting these workers to perform useless tasks and use scarce resources in so doing?

The Census Bureau spokesman has the priorities reversed— the benefits are long term (fifty years or more) and the problems are short term (ten years or less). But I am sure his time spans are different from mine. Unfortunately, no one wants to look at really long-range problems. Most people think that everything over six months is long term. One may be considered a little kooky even to have a thought about what might happen ten years hence.

What Is "Job Philosophy"?

A year ago, Hawker Siddeley Group, Ltd, a large British airplane manufacturer, canceled final development and production of the HS-146, a new short haul jetliner, because too few orders for planes were in hand or prospect. The 400 planes they had hoped to build would have provided 20,000 jobs. Loud screams of "irresponsible wrecking tactics" came from union leaders and government officials, reflecting the belief that only the jobs were important, not what they produced.

How much work done in this country advances the purposes of a particular corporation or branch of government, but really does nothing positive to make life better, except for those who get paid to do the work? This question opens a Pandora's box. We recognize that such a question can begin to be answered only when we have some way of determining national and human goals, and identifying what needs to be done to achieve them.

When we stop to think, we recognize that some organizations with a payroll may be performing no function that really improves the quality of life in the country as a whole. They may merely be collecting revenue from the rest of the country (through sales, if a corporation, or taxes, if governmental) to distribute within their own community, creating little or nothing of value in the process. In fact, they do a great deal of work for nothing.

In all cases, job philosophy puts the interest of the individual or a particular small group above the interest of society as a whole, whether that society be the state, the nation, the consuming public, or workers in all groups other than the one in question. The general interest is not the same as the sum of all individual interests, nor is the individual better off if his particular job philosophy is recognized at the price of most other individuals having their job philosophy recognized as well.

This is obvious in a small and self-sufficient community. In the primitive tribe, each individual had a function essential to the tribe's survival: if he failed to perform it, the tribe could not carry his dead weight. Our affluent society can carry a heavy load of non-producers and even tolerate individuals who, deliberately or not, have a negative impact. But it cannot carry too great a load without serious effect on the economy as a whole. The growth of job philosophy to the point where a substantial proportion of our labor force, in both private industry and government, is engaged in tasks that are either unnecessary or counterproductive, is certainly a major reason for our present inflationary problem.

Obviously, to the extent that useless effort is being expended, the economy as a whole suffers. If each community is contributing to the support of other communities by purchases or payment of taxes without receiving value in return, it is worse off, unless, to the ultimate cost of every other community, it can wangle enough payroll proceeds into its own sphere to more than offset the losses.

In *The Riddle of the Pyramids*, Kurt Mendelssohn makes a fascinating analysis of why all the major Egyptian pyramids were built during a single century several thousand years B.C. An engineer, he did not begin his studies to find out why. His solution came from engineering insights that could hardly be expected of the archaeologists who, in their own way, had been seeking a solution to the riddle for more than a century.

Pyramids, like any building, are built, from the bottom up. But, because of their shape, as the top is neared, far fewer people can find space to work on the construction. But the Pharaohs did not want to send home half or three-quarters of a work force in the tens of thousands. It was more efficient to keep going, so they started another pyramid when the first one was done. One Pharaoh, Snofru, had three large pyramids built or well under construction during his reign. According to Mendelssohn,

> The pyramid project was creating a type of community which had never existed before. Tribal villagers were welded by common work into people with the consciousness of nationhood. It was probably for the first time that they thought of themselves first and foremost as Egyptians. Working together, under one administration, their differences and mutual suspicions were bound to lessen. With this unifying labour on three large pyramids in the reign of Snofru it may have become of secondary importance in which of them he was eventually buried. In fact, it was not even important whether his body was buried in any of his three pyramids. . . . Once it is realized that the main object of pyramid construction was a work programme leading to a new social order, the religious meaning and ritual importance of the pyramid recedes into the background. If anything, these man-made mountains are a monument to the progress of man into a new pattern of life, the national state, which was to become his social home for the next 5000 years.[1]

This was job philosophy in action at the dawn of civilization. The Pharaohs (and the powerful priesthood) made job philosophy work for them as a tremendous unifying force. The cathedral building of the eleventh century in Europe performed the same function. Many people think that the space program of the nineteen sixties had little other value (I disagree).

Job philosophy is with us everywhere we turn. "We need to build that new highway because of the employment it will provide." "We can't close the air base because of all the business it brings to the area." "We shouldn't buy a foreign car because it takes bread out of the mouths of American workers." It is job philosophy to require extra men on train crews, to require that electrical work done in the factory be pulled out and done over on the construction site, to insist that, even if only a fuse has to be changed, a registered electrician has to be called in to conform to union regulations. Going further, there is job philosophy in any work which does not improve the quality of life. Think of the gimmicky and junky products that no one would ever ask for if someone were not trying to make a buck. What about the washroom attendant who gives you a perfunctory brushdown for a tip? Our answer is: "He's just trying to earn a living." That should not be an acceptable answer.

Once one begins to brainstorm about what specific products or services really don't improve the quality of life, the list seems endless. Start thinking about this subject and you begin to realize that many of us work hard and get paid for contributing little or nothing to the quality of life, by almost any definition. Once one begins to play this game, it is endless. If the product you make or the service you perform is directed to other industries, to what extent are those other industries really improving the quality of life by what they produce.

How many products really contribute to the quality of life? Surprisingly few, if you are willing to take your analysis all the way. It is my personal opinion that much advertising performs no useful educational function, even when it peddles products that are in themselves useful. Take any magazine, run through the ads, and make your own judgment of their social utility. Even if the product advertised has value, few ads are truly enlightening, although occasionally they may entertain.

"But," you say, "if the magazine didn't print these advertisements, it would not have the funds to put out a magazine at all, and so the ads do serve a useful purpose." This is true, but it is only part of the story. Presumably, companies run advertisements because they believe that they will stimulate greater sales of their products, which they hope will produce more profits. Since the cost of ads is a tax deductible expense, and the Federal income tax rate for most corporations is 48%, Uncle Sam will receive 48¢ less in taxes for each dollar of the advertising expense of a profitable corporation. So the company starts out risking only 52¢ on the dollar.

Someone has to pay for this advertising. Usually the customer pays more because the price of the product has to include the cost of advertising. The taxpayer pays the rest to offset Uncle Sam's loss of revenue due to the advertising-expense deduction.

When a product is relatively new and market penetration is still necessary, advertising may pay for itself, if the greater sales it produces permit economies of scale in production and distribution that exceed the cost of the advertising.

If there are a number of companies competing in an established market, however, the companies may only be fighting for market share. Cigarette advertising is a classic example. The companies with well established brands reaped a bonanza when cigarette advertising on TV was banned, because they no longer had to spend vast sums to counteract the ads of their competitors. Many people thought the money saved would be diverted to advertising in other media. It was not. The money saved provided much of the financial muscle for the tobacco companies to diversify into new fields. Yet, without any TV advertising and despite strong health campaigns against cigarettes, sales of cigarettes have actually gone up. Knowing this, we may wonder what possible function the TV ads performed.

Let us return to the argument that ads make the magazine (or the TV program) possible. We now see that, except for ads which pay for themselves by increasing market size, the customers for the products advertised share the cost almost equally with the taxpayers as a whole. Thereby, the two groups subsidize the magazine so that it can be sold at a much lower price than if it had no ads at all. Advertising is thus a clumsy device for redistributing values from product customers and taxpayers on one side to magazine readers on the other (with advertisers, publishers, printers, paper and ink suppliers, and a host of others all taking a profit cut from the transaction). All of this results in considerable waste of energy and resources in the total labor and materials which it takes to make the complex system work. I come to the disheartening conclusion that a very small part of the expense in materials and labor in creating and publishing advertising has any value to the economy as a whole. Rather, it is another drag.

Or take steel. The fact that a certain number of people are required to make so many tons of steel does not mean that their jobs are necessary. One must analyze what the tons of steel will be used for—to the extent that useless products cease to be made, so will the steel to make them. For example, if autos become smaller, we will need less steel.

We all have our special candidates for products the world could do without. My number one choice is the motorized tierack. I am sure each person will have a prize example. There are plenty of them. A generation ago, who would have dreamed that a company listed on the New York Stock Exchange could thrive doing nothing but helping people prepare their income tax returns? In the context of the benefit to the total society, this seems like the ultimate in futile activity, not that the individual doesn't need tax guidance, but that the society should be so structured that it is necessary.

The often-heard argument that we cannot expand mass transit at the expense of auto transportation because of the jobs that will be lost is obviously false reasoning. In the context of today's political climate, however, it carries considerable weight. We should recognize that this is just one more form of job philosophy. We should address ourselves to solving our real problem, not to trying to cure the symptoms.

Today, a large part of the work performed is unnecessary, although many people putting out a great deal of effort would object violently to being told their work had no inherent value except to provide their own income. So long as they get paid, probably most people don't care. I refer not just to the employee but also to the employer. Now that we are aware of the necessity of energy and resource conservation, we also know that doing any unnecessary job that requires the use of energy or resources is not just useless, it damages all of us.

Thinking objectively about the companies you know and the products and services they provide can be both an eye-opening and a chastening experience. Fortunately for our sanity, most of us can live on two mental planes at one time and in addition are expert rationalizers.

Job philosophy applies primarily to the employment of individuals, but the definition should be stretched to include any business activities which use precious energy to provide useless goods or services.

Competition is the motivating engine of capitalism. Genuine competition is not wasteful, because it stimulates constant improvements in quality and service. A generation ago, certain economists touting the presumed virtues of socialism used the example of the capitalistic competitive waste of having several milk companies provide home delivery in the same area, each driver competing with the others for a share of the business whereas, in a socialist world, one driver could handle all the customers himself. Home delivery of milk and cream has now almost disappeared, partly because of high labor costs and partly because modern refrigeration permits longer storage times, so it no longer has to be rushed from the cow direct to you. Most of us go to the supermarket to pick up dairy products.

But the example is still pertinent. If one company has a monopoly in an area, free from competition, there is little incentive to provide decent service or good quality, and certainly it can charge more. Since milk is a necessity for some people, active competition is essential to protect the customer from exploitation.

Our modern developed society has broadened the meaning of competition. In the developed world, where income is more than adequate to take care of the bare necessities of life (although we consider many luxuries of a generation ago to be necessities today), the discretionary dollar can be spent in many ways—for a case of beer, a new book, a set of coffee cups and saucers, or whatever you choose. A manufacturer of a product has to show not only that it is better than the products of its direct competitors but that it is more desirable than anything else that the buyer might want at the time.

Therefore, reducing the number of competitors who supply a particular product does not necessarily lessen the competition for the customer's money. Even if there is a monopoly or near-monopoly in a particular item, effective competition exists to the extent that something other and different is available to the potential customer as an equally attractive alternative.

I am a firm believer in anti-trust legislation, particularly as it applies to the basic industries which supply the necessities of life. Monopoly of a luxury product, however, doesn't bother me, because the easy recourse of the consumer is not to buy it at all. I believe, therefore, that as we move towards more regionalized (localized) economies the resulting reduction in the number of effective competitors need not reduce the effectiveness of capitalism.

Job philosophy has another unfortunate effect that needs mention. It leads to shortsighted policies for resource management. The conservationists who seek to save the redwoods from continued clear cutting run into the argument that to stop cutting down these trees will cost jobs.

A lumber company has to keep on cutting to have anything to sell. If it is to make money this year, it has to cut as fast and as economically as possible. Although the lumber company manager may personally be more interested in company sales and profits than in the number of people employed, trying to save these jobs enlists labor support. The lumber companies don't seem to be concerned that the big trees will all be gone in fifteen to twenty years at present cutting rates. If they do keep cutting, what will happen to the jobs then? No one knows. In any event, that is fobbed off as the problem of the next generation.

In the same way, job philosophy is a main argument in favor of most resource development projects. This is another instance in which the market discounts future benefits so heavily that they weigh no more than a feather in comparison with cash income today.

If employment were not the principal means of allocating

income, saving of jobs would not be so weighty an argument. We would be better able to weigh the tradeoffs between present convenience and future benefits in using or saving a resource. We would avoid the unfortunate but understandable bias of the employees whose livelihoods depend upon obtaining the utmost economic benefit right now. Requiring the preparation of environmental-impact statements is certainly a heavy burden added to already burdensome costs of exploiting resource opportunities. Those who believe in unending growth will always argue that such statements are not only unnecessary, but are roadblocks to progress. Progress to what? That is less clear.

As a nation, we could afford job philosophy so long as it was a minor fraction of our employment. A rich, abundant economy can carry this hidden load without difficulty. In fact, in an expanding world, we pay an insignificant penalty for job philosophy. But in a no-growth or slow-growth society, the incubus becomes too big. Full employment is achieved at the price of supporting a large population of our workforce who contribute little or nothing and waste precious fuel energy so doing.

Where does all this leave us? If, as I believe, a large proportion of the so-called productive effort of our system produces little or nothing of real value to human life, what can be done? Are we not hopelessly trapped in an economic system which has us struggling harder for survival than we need to?

Trapped, yes; hopelessly, no. The first step, I believe, is to recognize what is happening. When we see featherbedding, planned obsolescence and useless products or services, let us label them "job philosophy." The ancient Egyptians had the advantage that all their job philosophy was concentrated in one glorious project and, when the doing of it ceased to have moral value, they phased it out in a very short time. Today, our boondoggles are so numerous and so varied, and so often well disguised by the complications of our system, that we can't identify them and we have no idea how pervasive they are.

Job philosophy serves no purpose except a clumsy and wasteful method of redistributing income. Yet it is so widespread that it is hard to pin down what total price we are paying. Once a system is set up so that we can scarcely know how to function without it, our thinking is more and more directed toward providing employment as such. We show little concern about the real value of what the employees produce. Why else do we permit featherbedding which adds to the cost and effort it takes to make a product, while at the same time we count on planned obsolescence to be sure that the product doesn't last too long?

In essence, providing employment has become the principal justification for paying many of those who otherwise might be unemployed and, therefore, destitute. The demand for employment is not an expression of a desire to work; it is a demand for a share of the nation's income. Employment now serves as the principal means of income distribution. If capitalistic enterprise cannot provide *productive* employment for all who seek work in order to get their share of that income, the people will seek jobs anyway because they must have income to live and will not care whether the jobs produce anything or not. That is how job philosophy starts.

Job philosophy is not a capitalistic phenomenon. On the contrary, a relatively free enterprise system in its growth years has room for little or no job philosophy. The entrepreneur has every incentive to insure that the enterprise and all its employees are fully productive. It is only when controls begin to be applied to the unrestrained operation of capitalism that job philosophy begins to appear.

Automation is in one way the father of job philosophy. When the manufacturer, using automation, can produce goods at a lower price, those who thereby become unemployed cease to be able to buy them. I am not arguing that automation creates unemployment in itself. Often, it makes possible the production of goods or services which could not otherwise be created at all. But usually it disrupts employment patterns, at least temporarily.

Since employment is our principal method of income distribution, when business can no longer supply jobs, government must do so. It is no accident that almost one third of our total work force is employed by various governments, federal, state and local, and that a vast number of other jobs exist only to supply government.

If automation is the father of job philosophy, by making it possible to have a prosperous society without everyone working, bureaucracy is the mother who nourishes it from day to day. Although the labor union movement has its share of responsibility for job philosophy, without the support of bureaucratic government the impact would have been small.

In a bureaucracy, pay, status, and power are achieved not by personal accomplishment toward the goals of the total organization, but by political maneuvering within the hierarchy. Decay inevitably follows.

In the United States, a substantial percentage of people still care what their work produces. So long as and to the extent that they do, the job will somehow get done. But the trend is against us. If few people care about what is achieved, but only want to be sure that they retain a paying job, the economy cannot survive indefinitely.

In Italy today, the economy is awash in a rampant bureaucracy. In trying to give jobs to everyone to solve unemployment, the government is insuring that less and less will be accomplished. One commentator describes an example in point:

> . . . Italy's perennial poverty incites authorities to insist on written documentation of the simplest procedures, often a stamped paper. Stamps are a way of collecting some taxes from a nation of tax evaders.
>
> Such over-documentation leads to absurdities. To borrow a book from Rome's new national library, one must fill out first a form in duplicate to enter the building, then a form in triplicate for each book required. Then, one must go to the Bank of Italy, miles away, and start a whole new bureaucratic procedure for the payment of a deposit. Then one returns and, strikes permitting, receives a book.
>
> All this form-filling boosts employment, an important consideration in a country with chronic unemployment.[2]

Job philosophy has run wild in Italy. Chaos will inevitably be followed by economic collapse unless the country is able to recognize that what is achieved by the workers is ultimately more important than the number of jobs that can be created. Sooner or later, we must all take the same lesson to heart.

In our U.S. economy, once a job has been established, whether it performs any social purpose or not, the jobholder has a vested interest in its perpetuation. A company whose business is helping people prepare their tax returns is necessarily opposed to any simplification of taxes that will make its service less necessary. Trial lawyers are opposed to no-fault insurance because they have a vested interest in litigation, regardless of the social chaos the litigation may cause. Likewise, they have opposed no-fault divorce for obviously self-serving reasons. Every government bureau has a vested interest in its own continuance and violently opposes any reduction of its activities. The trucking industry wants authority to carry heavier and heavier loads, regardless of how much these loads break up the highways. The billboard lobby is opposed by almost everyone except the politicians who need low-cost or free personal exposure on billboards before each election.

Continued job philosophy is a form of creeping paralysis, from which we all suffer, although we are scarcely aware of it. It is a hidden tax on everything we buy. So long as a high rate of unemployment is politically unacceptable, we know that we have to carry the deadweight of people who do not produce. We compound our problem, however, by expecting from them work which uses precious energy and resources to no purpose.

In a technological society full employment and freedom from inflation are basically incompatible. So long as the United States economy grew rapidly, as it did for most of its history, substantially full employment could be achieved without inflation because the continual increase in population supplied the increasing market for all the additional goods a burgeoning technology could provide. An uneasy balance in the economy could be maintained, so that inflationary increases in prices could be kept moderate and unemployment kept below 5%.

Recently other factors have added to inflationary pressures. Union insistence on higher wage levels has effectively prevented the reduction in costs which would be expected in a free economy when supply of goods exceeds demand. Since wages stay up and even climb in times of oversupply, price reductions are rare. As wages are forced up, prices generally follow, unless the sellers need the business so badly that they will sell at the same or lower prices regardless of cost. The expectation of continued inflation is another influence which encourages people to buy more today at high prices in order to avoid paying even higher prices tomorrow.

When an economy slows up or ceases to grow, either because population begins to level off or because conservation of energy and resources requires a slowdown, the inherent incompatibility of full employment and freedom from inflation becomes apparent. An American Electric Power Company ad campaign has stressed that energy conservation generates massive unemployment. This is clearly true. The assumption, however, is that the problem is avoidable. It is not. Arguing that energy must be supplied to keep people employed is merely job philosophy in a different guise.

If we understand that many jobs are performed merely to provide employment and not because of what the workers may produce in goods or services, we may also wonder whether there are not better ways of distributing income than via the paycheck. The work itself seems to confer no benefit on the worker. It is done just to keep the individual occupied and presumably out of mischief.

While our highly technological economy is growing slowly or not at all, if we insist on having full employment, we are insuring rapid increase in prices. There is no escaping this. You may blame it on the government, blame it on business, blame in on anybody. You would do as well to blame the sun for not shining at night.

What Is "Job Philosophy"?

The increasing necessity to conserve energy and resources not only in the United States, but worldwide, will force us to face this problem squarely. If we buy small cars instead of big ones, there will be less employment in Michigan. Employment will drop even more as we gradually switch to mass transit to save precious energy. We will be less able to shift our labor force to building new products to meet new and expanded wants, because much such production would use energy and resources which will become far too expensive. We must become increasingly skilled, however, in making intelligent tradeoffs by deciding which wants we can afford to satisfy.

Each recent government administration has learned what a struggle it is to achieve at the same time the politically desirable goals of full employment, on one hand, and little or no inflation, on the other. When employment is high, everyone has money to spend and wants to buy goods and services at the very time when there is not enough productive capacity to make the things they want. Scarcity drives up prices, causing inflation. On the other hand, when *un*employment is high, there is less money to buy goods, so that, with less demand, in a free market, prices will tend to drop or, at least, not climb. Thus, inflation is less likely to occur when many people are out of work.

In a growth economy, we have learned that an uneasy balance can be maintained between moderately high employment and a modest rate of inflation by making the total economic machine run faster and faster. The hope is that everyone will believe they are better off because they are making more money, and won't be too aware that they are getting less for it. We are beginning to learn how illusory this is, without knowing what we can do about it. If an important function of growth is to make it possible to maintain the precarious balance of simultaneous high employment and low inflation, sooner or later something has to give, particularly if fuel and resource scarcities become common.

In a steady-state economy the escape valve of growth would not exist, and the basic incompatibility of full employment and lack of inflation would become more apparent. In a non-growth world, there would be no need to build new facilities to take care of population growth. When population levels out, school and housing construction efforts will be turned to maintaining and upgrading old facilities, not building new ones. In a world of limited resources, we will have to make do with what we have, except to the extent that necessary new products use less energy than the old. Products will have to be made to last a long time and built-in obsolescence will be taboo. Conspicuous consumption of all kinds will disappear. For instance, our peculiarly American potlatch ceremony of bestowing expensively wrapped presents on our family and friends at Christmas time will have to be modified, if only to reduce the waste of packaging. Keeping up with the Joneses will have to take new directions, not involving use of scarce energy in the form of material goods or services. Frugality will once more become a virtue.

But even today, in a growth economy, if we eliminated all the activities that make no contribution to improving our quality of life, we might well cut employment in half. In a steady-state world, even less employment would be needed. Thus, the job philosophy problem could be even more aggravated.

Is there a cure for job philosophy or do we have here a basic dilemma to which there is no clear answer? It is easy to say that jobs are a poor way to distribute income, but what is the alternative? When jobs are hard to get and hold, as they have been in most of the past few decades, job philosophy thrives. When the supply of goods is greater than the demand, two groups press for production, whether there is a ready market or not, the workers who need the security of a job and the companies that need to make a profit.

Can we eliminate job philosophy without undercutting our whole system of rewards and incentives? In a steady-state world, less work will be required for two reasons:

1 As population growth slows up, there will be less need to build homes, schools, factories, new highways and all the thousand items which depend upon growth. We are experiencing this already, although the trend is still not clear. The capital goods and construction industries (and those depending on them) will suffer disproportionately.

2 Sooner or later, energy shortages will become more severe. Fossil fuel energy has already soared in price. With energy scarce and expensive, we will not be able to produce some goods economically. Even when production is highly automated, employees are needed for management, maintenance, delivery, and distribution. Eliminating products will inevitably eliminate jobs.

One way to eliminate job philosophy is to remove enough people from the labor market so that there are scarcely enough people available to supply the basic goods and services without which we revert to a much poorer life. If available labor were scarce (and if everyone agreed that it would continue to be so), the worker would become a precious asset no longer needing union protection to insure job security, and would not have to featherbed or loaf to keep the job from running out. The employer would have his hands full producing goods and services for which there is a strong demand. Therefore, he wouldn't bother with making things for which a demand had to be artificially created. He would be less interested in cornering a larger market share, because, if a more efficient competitor preempted one market, there would be plenty of other markets for the taking.

There will be three trends that will tend to reduce job philosophy, however:

1　Because of the cost of energy, there will be a shift from energy-intensive to labor-intensive activities, which will require more human work. A sharp and permanent increase in the need for labor is one way to sop up the supply. The increasing cost of fuel energy may solve the unemployment problem by making the use of labor more economical as a partial substitute for energy-intensive technology. In fact, after the first disruptions of employment are worked through, job philosophy might be substantially reduced by the energy crunch.

　　The theory has been that automation improves efficiency so much that it makes possible the doing of new tasks which could not be done at all before, thus satisfying new wants and thereby creating new jobs to replace those lost to the machine. This is often (although not always) true. But many machines use inordinate amounts of increasingly expensive fuel energy, so that automation may be less economic in the future than in the past.

　　If we return to a more labor-intensive society,

many people will be needed to work with their muscles to replace some machine work. Service industries will thrive, because they require less resources and less non-renewable energy. But such modifications in our system may only partly fill the employment gap, for we will still use substantial fuel energy. There is no foreseeable need to return to the kind of primitive, completely labor-intensive economies we find in the less-developed nations.

2 To the extent that there is a trend toward smallness of activity (smaller companies, smaller market areas, smaller governmental units) more human effort will be needed even though the elimination of the diseconomies of scale may minimize this effect.

Available fuel energy will call the turn. Since transportation is one of our largest energy users, its high costs will begin to offset the economies of scale of producing for an entire national (and international) market in a single giant plant or complex. Products with a high weight-to-cost ratio will be particularly affected because of the heavy transportation expense both to bring the materials to the central plant and to distribute the resulting goods to wide market. Smaller, decentralized operations will become competitive for many products, such as automobiles, heavy machinery, building products, steel, aluminum, and non-ferrous metals. We can, therefore, anticipate a major trend toward smaller, more independent communities, and a gradual slowing-up of the urbanization of the past century.

3 The gradual changeover to energy sources other than

oil will be capital-intensive. The development of different aspects of solar power will require tremendous investments in facilities and equipment. Necessarily, the construction of these facilities will require vast amounts of fuel energy, which will squeeze our available supplies even more.

Some of the necessary tradeoffs between energy and labor may be hard. As an example, the farmer in India now puts in almost 100 times as much labor as the American per kilocalorie of wheat protein produced, and yet uses almost 20% as much fossil energy.[3] If it requires 100 times more labor to save only 80% of the fossil energy, we face a terrible problem, unless we can strike a better balance at a less primitive level. Almost certainly we can, although there is no assurance of it.

How the job philosophy problem will be met depends on which trends develop first. The three trends listed above may not in themselves solve the job philosophy and accompanying unemployment problems. We will need additional ideas, at least for the transition period.

Two additional means of reducing the pressure for jobs suggest themselves, but they will require legislative action: public works, and a guaranteed annual income.

There are many necessary jobs which involve a product or service that people don't buy directly. Our governments already supply many products and services in this category, from highway construction to police protection. As federal, state, and local governments have taken on more and more tasks, they have grown so big that they now employ over a third of our total work force. Although government activities are inefficient and often counterproductive, there are some really valuable public works that they could undertake. We must, however, avoid creating jobs merely to keep people busy. Instead, we could initiate meaningful progress to improve our cities and towns—no one will question that there is room for improvement.

We all know that there is an almost infinite amount of work to be done to improve our lives and our quality of life, some of which requires little or no fuel-energy expenditure. So long as our units of responsibility are so large—a vast Federal government or a giant multinational corporation—we are naturally reluctant to entrust the performance of these many local and often simple and obvious tasks to entities so large that beneficial programs get swamped in bureaucratic inefficiency and corruption.

As only one example, a program launched by the Federal government with even so laudable a purpose as Head Start soon became lost in the bureaucratic jungle and largely benefited the leeches who bled it for every cent they could. Some benefit does trickle down to the children, but very little.

When the unit of organization is small, however, so that we can identify and know personally the people who will be responsible for performance, we can tackle these *pro bono publico* tasks more effectively. The smaller the geographical scope of the program and its management, the better chance it has for success. High visibility is prerequisite to effective supervision. When the scope of operation is necessarily small, the communications improve immensely. Smaller is clearly better.

The movement toward smallness must be an all-inclusive one, not just an arbitrary reduction in unit size in the government aspect of our world. Small governmental units will not give us the benefits of smallness when those who make up its constituency either work outside the area or are employed by organizations of great scope which are not primarily interested in the welfare of the particular community.

There will be a trend toward smaller, more independent and self-sufficient economic, social and political communities, and this will be beneficial to us all. Although some of the economies of scale may be lost by reducing the size of market for particular products and services, this will be more than made up by:

1   Reduction in the diseconomies of scale, particularly by improving intra-organizational communications;
2   Reduction in job philosophy by spotlighting its costs and fallacies;
3   Encouraging community (local government) assumption at the local level of many tasks which, when tried on a national scale, collapse in bureaucratic ineptitude.

Public works can absorb vast numbers of workers and thereby reduce the pressure to hang on to meaningless jobs. Among the problems, however, will be to make these projects attractive enough to draw people out of industry, and secure enough so they will be willing to undertake them, yet still demanding enough so the public as a whole will really benefit from what is done. I believe, this is possible only under the scrutiny provided in a localized community.

Another approach is a guaranteed annual income, assured to everyone who wants it, regardless of need.[4] GAI is not the equivalent of, nor a substitute for, welfare. The payment of a guaranteed annual income is in consideration of a benefit received or to be received in the future, largely in the form of improvement in the education, capacity, or special talents of the recipient. Welfare has no *quid pro quo*.

But what would the person on GAI do? Warren A. Johnson suggests:

> A guaranteed income . . . could perform three important functions. It could expand the opportunities for public service, (2) support the development of new methods of livelihood appropriate to an age where it is no longer necessary or even useful for everyone to have an economically efficient job, and (3) it could discourage economic growth while still providing a flexible device for maintaining the stability of our economic system.[5]

Although this may be seen as a form of welfare, GAI is really an environmental measure, because, by removing people from the job market, it would discourage the non-essential, polluting, and energy-wasting production that costs so much.[6]

The problem of GAI is control. We see nothing wrong in supporting people doing work which has no immediate economic value but benefits the society as a whole. But we may object to supporting them in idleness or doing things they may deem important but society does not. Because the control problem is so serious, we must approach GAI with extreme caution. If our civilization turns to smaller entities (business, governmental and societal), control will become much easier, and we will be able to adapt our programs more skillfully to local needs and problems.

While the provision of a guaranteed annual income would encourage a substantial proportion of the people to abandon employment, thus eliminating job philosophy by tightening the labor market, I find it unpalatable as the sole solution because of: 1) its high, probably prohibitive, cost, 2) its susceptibility to abuse, particularly if operated like most large scale government programs; 3) the implication that those who still work have to take care of those who choose not to.

In the limited environment of a small community, however, I would be happy to see some proportion of our people freed from the obligation to earn a living in order to devote themselves to pursuits for which there can be no assigned dollar value but which could (or might) benefit the community as a whole. In a small self-sufficient community, we have a far better chance to watch and see how our money is spent.

But we may not be able to wait until we reach the smaller society. We may need GAI long before then. With all its problems, we must keep GAI in our kit of tools and be ready to consider it sooner if we must. We may never need it. More likely, it will be a transitional device.

As we move to smaller and less automated and necessarily more labor-intensive operations, employment opportunities will expand and the present trend to eliminate human labor will be reversed. Unless we seek the totally automated society in which each of us will be wrapped in our own cocoon without the need to do anything, this should be a far healthier world. The pressure of a generation ago to continue shortening the work week seems to have diminished, partly because so many people have had to moonlight on a second job to make ends meet, but partly also because we do not seem psychologically to be able to stand too much leisure.

Elimination of job philosophy may be the natural corollary of the changes an energy-expensive society will bring upon us anyway. We will have a difficult transition, however, because of the major adjustments we will have to make in our economic system all at one time. Some of us who are able to look beyond our own special interest will realize that the best course for the country will inevitably result in our own economic interests being severely hurt. But if we consider the alternatives, we may conclude that, in the long run, we and our children will be better off putting our general interest in the economy as a whole ahead of our special interest in the particular economic entities that provide us a living.

We can hardly expect such altruistic conduct to be normal, however. Nor need we. We can expect that managerial bureaucracy in both big business and government will oppose change to the death. But economic compulsions will be direct and immediate and we will have to respond. If we understand what is happening, it will be far easier to direct our economy through this immensely difficult period, both as individual businessmen and as citizens.

6

Why Do We Work?

WHAT ABOUT THE PURITAN WORK ETHIC which seems to be an essential element of our culture? Isn't work a necessary part of our lives? Yes, but the work ethic itself is relatively new. The Puritans absorbed the work ethic from Calvinism, a particularly strict expression of Protestantism which originated in the early sixteenth century. Before then, mankind survived for countless thousands of years without any deepfelt necessity to acquire virtue by hard work.

In the Bible, work was deemed a curse, not a blessing (Genesis iii: 19). In the sixteenth century John Calvin created the work ethic. In his words, "labor is a thing so good and Godlike . . . that makes the body hale and strong and cures the sicknesses produced by idleness . . . In the things of this life, the laborer is most like to God." The idea of one's "calling" comes from Calvinism. To the Calvinist, the "calling" is not a condition to which the individual is born, but a strenuous and exacting enterprise to be chosen by himself, and to be pursued with a sense of religious repsonsibility.[1]

Why Do We Work?

In a predestinarian religion such as Calvinism, stressing the virtue of economic labor sanctified singleminded attention to business. The Protestant church was a powerful ally of the businessman who needed willing and submissive workers. In addition, predestinarianism tended to glorify success in business as evidence that the businessman, by virtue of his very success, must be one of the predestined few chosen for salvation. The Calvinist businessman who assumed that he was one of the predestined elect had a sort of logic which said: "Since I am predestined to be saved, whatever I do, being predestined, is good in the sight of God; therefore, whatever I do for the good of the business is good in the sight of God, too." He entered a kind of partnership with God, in which the humility of the Middle Ages was considerably watered down.

The creation of the so-called work ethic in the sixteenth century had the long-run effect of separating economic from religious life and leaving the former freed from the constraints of the latter. The work ethic can be seen as a special device to provide the moral compulsion to work essential to the development of the Industrial Revolution and its expansion throughout the world. "Progress" and "religion" went hand in hand. Not only that, it gave the workers

> the comforting assurance that the unequal distribution of the goods of this world was a special dispensation of Divine Providence. . . . Calvin himself had made the much-quoted statement that only when the people, i.e., the mass of laborers and craftsmen, were poor did they remain obedient to God.[2]

For primitive man and earlier civilized man, work as such was not a virtue. Rather than work hard, man worked as little as possible and settled for a limited standard of living. Richard Wilkinson, in a startling and convincing book, argues that economic development arose only when the ecological equilibrium was upset by excessive pressures on available resources because of population growth. To quote him:

> Development comes out of poverty, not out of plenty as many economic theories would lead one to suppose. Poverty stimulates the search for additional sources of income and makes people willing to do things they may previously have avoided. [3]

He also argues persuasively that most of the economic progress of which we are so proud actually results in a lower quality of life than was available to everybody when population was smaller. While he does not recommend that we return to a primitive way of life, he insists that it was an easier and, in many ways, a better life. We are reminded of the recent argument that, if we count the number of hours of work it takes to pay for an auto and to pay the costs of keeping it going, and divide them into the average number of miles driven, most of us could walk the same distance in the time spent. Anyway, was the trip necessary in the first place?

We should not disdain today's lifestyle in the less-developed world just because it is far simpler. The increasing complexity of our industrial structure is largely necessary, not because our way of life is better, but because, as population soars upward, it is the only way we can keep so many people alive in a limited world.

Working in our modern economic society is an acquired taste. The tyranny of the clock is hard to adjust to. But without careful scheduling and promptness, most businesses can't function. Many jobs in the office and on the factory floor are dull, menial, and repetitive, even though the percentage of varied and interesting jobs is gradually increasing as machines do more of the unskilled and semi-skilled work. As Richard N. Goodwin has said:

> Work is largely a process in which the individual exchanges his humanity for unhuman rewards. He comes to believe in the worth, even the necessity, of the money and position which are the object of his toil. . . When work is more than a work, when it becomes a system of belief, it cannot readily be laid aside. The leisure hours become an extension of the working day.[4]

Capitalism thrives on frenzied energy. The pressures built up in modern big business show that intense competition still is the rule within companies and between companies. Anyone who says competition has been superseded by monopoly has not witnessed corporate in-fighting in big business. The need for success, both individual and corporate, takes precedence over all other considerations. Competitive capitalism is a jealous god—it demands total devotion.

As one rises in the corporate hierarchy, growth itself becomes exciting and absorbing. We are caught up in it. No wonder life outside the business world often suffers by comparison. Most managers enjoy the process so much that it never occurs to them to wonder what they are doing or why. One is in the clothing game or the advertising game—it truly is a game, and, like children, many of us revel in it.

The businessman is often too exhausted by the strains of holding the business structure together to have any time for his family or life outside the corporate cocoon. Our young people of today have reacted strongly against their parents' intense concentration on business success. Some of them have totally condemned production because it required impersonal machines and coordinated effort; they have dropped out. Eventually, most of them learn that, without industrial production, the world cannot support us even in poverty. Most young people eventually turn to the business world to survive—and even to prosper. They are swept into the competitive maelstrom—and eventually become addicted to the work process, too.

The number of hours worked is no measure of accomplishment, particularly at the management level. Arriving at the office ahead of the boss and leaving for home after he leaves may be good evidence of your dedication, and often earns a raise or promotion, but it has little to do with whether the job is better done. When life is well paced and well rounded, more is accomplished in less time and with less effort.

I remember a carpenter we employed who never seemed to make any effort at all. He moved so deliberately that it was easy to believe he was malingering. Yet he never made a false move. When he drove a ten penny nail, he hit it four times and it was flush. Walls and doors and cabinets seemed to grow before your eyes, without any sensation of movement. I consider him a model of how to work.

Work should be enjoyed, but not just because we know nothing else. Business is challenging and exciting, particularly when it is most demanding, but it should never be our whole life.

In order to be absorbing, work has to seem to be worth doing. Perhaps workers are so often unhappy not because of the impersonality of the company and the monotony of their jobs, but because they sense that it doesn't really matter whether the job is done or not. A young person working on an assembly line producing large automobiles is aware that one more car isn't going to make American life any better for anyone but the man who eventually buys it. In fact, the car buyer benefits at the expense of the rest of us. Because that someone buys and uses the car, the rest of us will have that much less road and parking space and that much more air and noise pollution, all at the cost of using up more irreplaceable resources of metal, plastics, and gasoline. So a thoughtful young worker may wonder why he should work on it at all.

Is not this malaise the root of many of our social problems today? When it is obvious that a large proportion of the available jobs have no conceivable useful purpose, how can we help but be disillusioned about our society? Our fathers did useful work and were proud of it; many of us are merely placeholders. Although many employees find stimulation and satisfaction in their jobs, many others have none. Spiritual erosion is the result, more perhaps than we realize.

What is the function of work in human life? Work should have more meaning than the production of goods or services. But as E.F. Schumacher says,

> the modern economist has been brought up to consider labour or work as little more than a necessary evil . . . the ideal from the point of view of the employer is to have output without employees, and the ideal from the point of view of the employee is to have income without employment.[5]

When our system of enterprise puts all the emphasis on employment as a means of income and little or none on employment for other purposes (including how people may fulfill themselves in work), we are in trouble. Job philosophy, now that it has reached mammoth proportions, is a symptom of deep sickness. People need meaningful employment.

E.F. Schumacher describes the Buddhist philosophy of work:

> The Buddhist point of view takes the function of work to be at least threefold: to give a man a chance to utilize and develop his faculties; to enable him to overcome his ego-centredness by joining with other people in a common task; and to bring forth the goods and services needed for a becoming existence.[6]

The development of increasingly sophisticated machinery has enabled us to ease tremendously the drudgery and physical struggle of much human labor. No longer do we dig ditches by hand, struggle behind the horse-drawn plow, or swing a hammer to forge hot metal into shape. Present worker concern with the boredom and meaninglessness of factory work is in itself evidence of our success in making work less backbreaking. When work is utterly exhausting, there is no time to be bored.

Swedish auto makers Saab and Volvo have attempted to make production line jobs more interesting to the worker by setting up small work groups performing rotating tasks to provide greater variety and stimulation. Visting Americans have been favorably impressed, although a group of six American auto workers who worked four weeks at Saab under a Cornell University project had mixed feelings. One reaction was: "Working with a team, a few members of the group discovered, required accommodating themselves to others; they preferred to be responsible only for themselves'' (*Time*, March 10, 1975, p. 42).

The Japanese companies which have begun manufacture in the United States have imported from the homeland their deep concern for group awareness. As one practice, managers are expected to spend some time in menial tasks to promote group solidarity (*Fortune*, March, 1975). American workers, with a strong individualistic tradition and an anti-management bias fostered by union intransigency, sometimes seem to be uncomfortable in work situations requiring mutual cooperation. Giant American business has created this monster and is beginning to suffer the consequences. One of our great tasks is to make necessary work more meaningful partly by giving more substance to its possible group associations.

Much of the alienation between worker and management stems from a misapplication of supposed rules of efficiency. When management assumes that people do not want to work, they will tend to structure the job to treat the worker as a machine rather than as a human. The repetitive jobs of the automobile assembly line, for instance, are more suitable for robots than humans, as Charlie Chaplin demonstrated in Modern Times. Peter Drucker pointed out two decades ago that the one motion—one job concept (in which, if the process is divided into a number of components, each worker performs only one operation) is not the most efficient, even in the few industries where only one basically uniform product is made.

Drucker uses the surgeon as his best example of the worker who learns how to do each of the necessary steps in an operation with maximum skill and then performs the entire sequence himself.[7] The worker (in this case, the surgeon) has analyzed all the separate motions and put them together in an integrated whole, which best uses his uniquely human abilities. That is work in the best sense.

He makes another essential point:

> Wherever a job is too big, too complicated or too strenuous to be performed by an individual, it should be done by a community of individuals working as an organized team rather than by a series of individuals linked together mechanically. People who work together form a social group. They build personal relations over and above the work relationship.[8]

Work is a necessary element of all our lives. By definition, work is purposeful activity. By usage, in our civilization, work is what we do for a livelihood. Thus, carrying on a telephone conversation with a business associate is classified as work, while weeding one's own flower garden is leisure.

So long as we work in an office or a factory miles away from our home, work and leisure are clearly separated by the process of commuting daily from one to the other. Only the fortunate few can work at or near their homes, as was the almost invariable practice in our world a few generations ago.

One becomes aware of the difference between the old and the new in a Latin American city such as Buenos Aires. The Spanish custom of a three hour siesta during the hottest hours of the day, with working hours extended well into the cool of the evening, makes great sense in a small community where no one commutes. But in a modern city, where job and home are separated by a half hour or more of travel, commuting back and forth twice a day is an intolerable burden.

The solution is not to force the Latin Americans into our

mold. Our long range goal should be to bring work and play together once again in the home community so that they will merge more easily into each other, not only in Latin America, but in our developed world, too.

Work need not be for pay, although it almost always is. Money is useless except as a medium of exchange. Once we are aware at all times that it is not the money we desire but what the money will buy, we will also recognize that there are some things money can't buy for which we are willing to work.

Few people work solely for money, although most of us think we do. One former associate used to answer an employee's untimely request for a raise with the offer that he would be glad to find the employee a job somewhere else for higher pay if he really had to have more money. This was an effective ploy for dampening unreasonable expectations, because it made the employee ponder the special intangible benefits of the present job which he might not care to forfeit.

Which among the motivations that drive us can be harnessed effectively in a slow-growth or no-growth world? Douglas McGregor tells us that human needs are organized in a series of levels—"a hierarchy of importance." When bread is in short supply, man lives by bread alone. In our developed world, our physiological needs for bread are usually met, at least in the short run.

When our physiological needs are satisfied, the next level needs are the "safety needs"—"for protection against danger, threat and deprivation." The need is for the "fairest possible break." So long as employment is the principal means of determining the distribution of wealth, satisfaction of our "safety needs" calls primarily for job security. If being un-employed no longer entails financial disaster, as in a world where job philosophy is eliminated and paid employment is no longer the only way to earn a share of the wealth, the "safety needs" will be taken care of.

When the worker feels safe enough, the "social needs" become important, namely:

> . . . those for belonging, for association, for acceptance by one's fellows, for giving and receiving friendship and love. . . . Above the social needs—in the sense that they do not usually become motivations until lower needs are reasonably satisfied—are the needs of greatest significance . . . The egoistic needs.
>
> 1   Those that relate to one's self-esteem: needs for self respect and confidence, for autonomy, for achievement, for competence, for knowledge.
>
> 2   Those that relate to one's reputation: needs for status, for recognition, for appreciation, for the deserved respect of one's fellows.[9]

The Buddhist philosophy quoted above speaks primarily to the "social needs" as McGregor defines them. It ignores the egoistic needs, which provide much of the managerial motivation of a capitalistic society.

At the worker level, creating the atmosphere in which the social needs can be met is vitally important. If everyone in an organization is productive in one way or another, and knows it, morale is bound to be good. People like to work, if they are part of a well-functioning organization. When communications are good and morale is high, it is a pleasure to come to work. I was fascinated to read that Inland Container Corporation had seven goals for 1975 and that the seventh was "to have fun." A few others have said the same thing in more stilted terms. Enjoying work should be a basic goal, but few managers take it into account.

Good management knows how to structure the work environment to make it a pleasant place. Many companies, particularly smaller ones, do this very well. The work atmosphere is gradually improving.

We have much to learn, however, about how best to satisfy the "egoistic needs." Money is still our principal tool. It provides the proof of success which bolsters both our individual self-esteem and our reputation. Because of the anonymity of life in today's giant aggregations, money is the easiest way to provide the necessary ego-satisfactions, because it brings instant status which can be carried with you wherever you go.

Money incentives are powerful, but other incentives are necessary to make any society function. In the future, we will want to motivate with more direct ego-satisfaction than money. Financial rewards will necessarily be limited in an energy-scarce world so that we will have to learn how to use honors, prestige, publicity, and other non-financial benefits to do the job money does now. In a smaller, more intimate world, intangible rewards will carry more weight than they do now, because each person will be better known in the community where he both works and lives and will be evaluated for what he is and does, not just for how much money he can spend.

When we study the social life of primitive man we see that the moral influence of the family, the tribe, the sodality, and the band was dominant in insuring that conduct of the individual conformed with the standards and requirements of the group. Primitive societies were largely egalitarian in the distribution of their material output. Individual leadership and special merit were recognized, however, not only with prestige but materially. Yet such recognition was usually limited to the individual and did not endow the family with special status beyond the leader's life.[10]

There was a strong moral compulsion to act in the interests of the community as a whole. This still exists, although it seems almost lost in our giant anonymous society.

The American economic system has been outstandingly successful, not only because of its capitalistic structure, but also because of the silent and implicit pressure of the individual to be a good citizen. We tend to take this invisible force for granted. In fact, we deny its existence by attributing all work done for public purposes to capitalistic motives. If a shopkeeper sweeps the snow off the sidewalk in front of the store or cleans the debris out of the street gutters, we say that this is good for business, because it will attract more people into the store. If a metropolitan bank assigns an officer for an extended period to work in a charity drive, it is agreed that this is done in the hope of attracting new customers to the bank. We have grown ashamed or unwilling to admit that we have any motives other than materialistic ones.

Capitalism has always had a moral aspect. True, it is primarily individualistic and selfish and, in practice, has often been greedy. But underneath, there has been an awareness that the individual will benefit not just by exploitation but by providing goods and services the society needs. A tradition of pride in workmanship (perhaps inherited from the medieval guilds) has been an integral part of our economic system. Even Ayn Rand recognized this implicitly although denying that any motivation except self-interest had any place in a capitalist society.[11]

Bigness has eaten away at this tradition. It is not the bigness of the individual company, but the anonymity of our total society, that has made pride pointless. If a person works in one community for a company which spews its products all over the country (or the world), and lives in another area, loyalties are divided. Your residential neighbors have no way of knowing what you do for a living, far less whether your work is honest and good, and can value you only by how much money you seem to bring home.

In the giant corporate environment, there is great pressure to show financial results, and the top managers often don't know or care what corners must be cut to achieve them. Moral values often get only lip service. They are given attention only when they don't interfere with the basic concern of the company: making a bigger profit this year than last year.

A giant company may have many active and expensive programs to back socially beneficial institutions in its market area but, at the same time, may market products which it knows may have an eventual high social cost. DuPont, for example, one of the best-managed and most socially responsible large companies, continues to be the world's largest producer of fluorocarbons (its trademark is ''Freon'') for the refrigeration and aerosol industries, despite evidence that the fluorocarbons, when released into the atmosphere, eventually reach the protective ozone layer of our atmosphere and may attack and deplete it, with serious effects on human life and health. Its argument, of course, is that the case is not yet proven and it would be wrong to upset a major industry until it is. The problem is, however, that it takes many years for the gases to rise into the upper atmosphere, so that if all production of fluorocarbons were halted today, the effects on the ozone layer would still continue (and even increase) for many years. When we know the answer, it may well be too late.

Can you imagine a drug company today being permitted to market any medicine which has possible adverse side effects on a few users, before proper precautionary measures are clearly worked out? Perhaps the ozone peril is too remote to worry about as yet. I wonder.

Moral blindness is not a monopoly of big organizations. But there are fewer checks on it. The separation of ownership of the company from management has accentuated the problem. The owners have no necessary compulsion to maximize corporate-profit results at all costs; the managers do. Managers need profits *this year*; owners are concerned about the long-term results, which depend more on producing socially valuable goods and services, less on short-term manipulation.

We have all been contaminated a little. Too many of us act as if we believe that all that matters is personal material success. When, as a people, we ignore the effects of our actions on the greater community, we are insuring collapse of our civilization.

None of us is unselfish and civic-minded by nature. This social cohesion of the group depends upon each of us learning to participate actively in the life of the community. The social evolution of the human race depends upon the strength of the family and the associations which have grown from the family. Each of us is born utterly dependent on others for life and survival. Few animals require such careful nurture for so long a time. Every successful human society requires day-to-day mutually supportive cooperation of its members. We count on it. A few outlaws are enough to disrupt the whole community, unless immediate and effective steps are taken to control and isolate them.

Why Do We Work?

In a small, largely self-sufficient society, the moral compulsion is strong to do one's share in making the community function efficiently. Everyone is necessarily involved. In a small group, it is hard to avoid the pressures to conform to the group's image of what one should do, at risk of being subjected to scorn or even effective expulsion. (In ancient Greece, exile was considered a most painful penalty.)

Our present mass society has no such cohesion. While a person may gain some recognition because of leadership in the affairs of the community, if he chooses instead to do nothing, he will be left alone, but suffers no penalty.

Those employed by giant national and international companies move from city to city as their jobs require. They seldom develop the social ties necessary to bind them to the community. Their loyalty is to the companies which employ them and they have no compulsion to develop any other loyalties outside their own immediate family.

As our population has grown in numbers, as our cities have become bigger and more crowded, as our institutions have expanded into uncontrollable monstrosities, the place of the individual in society has been diminished. We really have become punchcards in an anonymous world, subject to being stapled, mutilated, and torn. We feel like flotsam on the tide of events.

Since we see our personal influence waning, it is not surprising that we have turned to government to take care of us. Government is remote and faceless, however. It intrudes in our lives coldly and demandingly, and when it tries to help, distributes its favors clumsily and unevenly. Even so, people rely on government to solve their problems, and that reliance is often the excuse to do nothing themselves.

No system can survive if a substantial percentage of the people think only of their immediate personal benefit without regard to the public good. Every building owner who burns down his building in order to collect the insurance damages us all. Every person who fails to come to the aid of a neighbor being robbed, because he doesn't want to get involved, is tearing down the only fabric that shields us from the jungle. We are approaching that jungle now.

It is true that the tyranny of the small group can be oppressive. We know that submission to the moral influence of the leadership in a small town, for instance, can be stultifying and even intimidating. The revolt against this kind of conformity finds expression in the desire to "do one's own thing," whatever it may be.

Complete independence from the influence of the society, however, weakens the society's structure. If all of us insist on "doing our own thing," there will be no structure at all. The implication is that each person can do what he or she most wants to do without relation to what needs to be done to keep the economy alive. I may not want to work in a steelmill, but some people must if we are to have all the products made of steel, from tin cans to bridges, which are important to our civilization. Work is necessary not just as a method of income distribution but to get things done. Sometimes we forget this.

Moral cohesion of the group is also necessary. If a society is to succeed, it must have a structure that its members accept, either expressly or implicitly. An economy cannot function without the acceptance of its rules of conduct by the overwhelming majority of its citizens, whether it is capitalistic or not.

What does all this say about job philosophy? Somehow, it

must be eliminated, because it corrupts our most basic principles. If you have ever known union members in totally useless jobs doing almost nothing (and sometimes even glorying in their uselessness), waiting out their time until retirement, you know that these are only empty shells of people, pitiful victims of extreme job philosophy. One's work must have purpose and meaning; without pride, we are nothing.

We must continue to work in one way or another; our nature requires it. The employment need not be for pay, however, in order to fulfill our social and egoistic needs. Human technological skills, even in a more labor-intensive society, will permit us to maintain a good material standard of living. In a world of smaller communities the quality of life will improve. Much routine and boring work will still have to be done; we will not always be able to "do our own thing." But we need not be total slaves to our jobs either. There is a middle way, and we must find it.

7

Can Capitalism Survive?

CAPITALISM IS A MARVELOUS SYSTEM, which has proved its capacity to "produce over time continuing improvement in the economic well-being of the masses of the people" (Joseph Schumpeter). The capitalist system, by its very nature, not only provides more riches to the few but brings all its benefits into the reach of all members of society.

Unfettered capitalism is indeed wonderful, but it is not an economic system for all situations. When the self-interest of the individual is generally parallel to the general interest, unrestricted capitalism works well. In a sparsely populated and underdeveloped economy, these conditions obtain. The economy benefits from the entrepreneurial activity of each individual capitalist who is propelled by his self-interest to make full use of the space and resources which he can control to produce goods and services the society needs and is willing to pay for. The more efficiently he and his competitors make use of the abilities and resources available to them, the more is produced at prices that are attractive to buyers. Everyone wins and prosperity increases.

The self-interest of the individual in his particular principal activity almost always outweighs his general and non-specific interest in the overall improvement in the life of society as a whole, even though he would be one of the beneficiaries of any such improvement. When the self-interest of the individual is not parallel to the general interest, therefore, problems arise because the individual pursues his self-interest at the expense of society as a whole.

When space or resources become limited, unrestrained competition for limited supplies of energy (or material) becomes not only wasteful but even destructive. In his essay, ''The Tragedy of the Commons,'' Garrett Hardin has shown precisely how and why this happens. If there are ten herdsmen with access to public pasture (a ''common'') which will support a hundred cattle without becoming overgrazed, and each of the ten herdsmen has ten cattle, the commons will receive full use, without exceeding the carrying capacity of the land. But that is only the beginning.

> As a rational being, each herdsman seeks to maximize his gain. Explicitly or implicitly, more or less consciously, he asks, ''What is the utility to *me* of adding one more animal to my herd?'' This utility has one negative and one positive component.

> 1   The positive component is a function of the increment of one animal. Since the herdsman receives all the proceeds from the sale of the additional animal, the positive utility is nearly $+1$.

2   The negative component is a function of the additional overgrazing created by one more animal. Since, however, the effects of overgrazing are shared by all the herdsmen, the negative utility for any particular decision-making herdsman is only a fraction of −1.

Adding together the component partial utilities, the rational herdsman concludes that the only sensible course for him to pursue is to add another animal to his herd. And another . . . But this is the conclusion reached by each and every rational herdsman sharing a commons. Therein is the tragedy. Each man is locked into a system that compels him to increase his herd without limit—in a world that is limited. Ruin is the destination toward which all men rush, each pursuing his own best interest in a society that believes in the freedom of the commons. Freedom in a commons brings ruin to all.[1]

Once we begin to apply Hardin's lesson to our world today, we see that in our finite world the commons include air, water, land, timber, minerals, fossil fuels, as well as living and working space itself. In addition, in Hardin's parable, we may recognize ourselves not only as the herdsmen but simultaneously as the cattle themselves gobbling up the resources which would be more than ample for a smaller population.

People, unlike cattle, are not satisfied with just enough grass for normal physical development: we have learned to be almost insatiable. This compounds our problem. If each individual consumes more and more, the number of people (cattle) that the world (the commons) can carry without overloading becomes smaller so that even if the population doesn't increase at all, we face the same tragedy.

Can Capitalism Survive?

What does this say about capitalism? To the extent that it permits the individual herdsman to continue to make his own free decision about how many cattle he will graze on the commons, it would seem that the eventual collapse of the system is assured.

But we must be very careful how we apply Hardin's rule. His parable assumes that the commons are precisely limited in their carrying capacity. He assumes, for instance, that there is no prospect either of improving the quality or amount of the grass on the commons or of developing breeds of cattle that require less forage, either of which would increase the commons's carrying capacity.

The issue of whether a given resource is limited in the sense that Hardin describes the commons is crucial to one's point of view about capitalism. People tend to think that there is a certain amount of wealth in the world and if one person becomes rich he does so by making one or more other people poor. In this view, life is treated as a zero-sum game in which the way the benefits are divided is the most important issue.

The incentives of capitalism, however, have stimulated us to ignore apparent limitation of resources so that we have often created new wealth where there was none before. Even though disproportionate rewards have been paid to those who direct the expansion of our economic world, the poorest among us are immensely better off materially than all but a few of the most fortunate individuals of a few generations ago.

Capitalist incentives have powered the Industrial Revolution lifting our standard of living immeasurably, not just by finding new space and new mineral and fuel resources, but by developing technology to make effective use of everything around us.

Wealth is created by the human brain, not just dug out of the ground.

But there are limits, and we are nearing a number of them. It is hard to pin down, however, when a particular limit will reached. If a particular resource such as tin, for example, becomes scarce and expensive, how can one tell whether new lodes of the mineral may be uncovered, or an acceptable and abundant substitute developed, or technological developments make it less essential to our economy? Capitalist incentives will continue to stimulate the implementation of all such alternatives.

I am not concerned about the lack of availability of specific resources, such as particular minerals. We will find substitutes or other answers. The continued problem of population, energy, and environment is far more formidable. There is no early answer. It is in this context that Hardin's parable has force, no matter how much we can mitigate its impact by further advances in technology.

We will be forced to turn to major conservation of energy. How can we do it? The first step is to eliminate waste, in one form or another. Adjusting the thermostat to 68°F in the winter and the air-conditioning to 74°F in the summer reduces energy consumption substantially without impairing the quality of life. The small car probably fulfills the same function as the large car for most people, and if we all use it, there is no apparent sacrifice. If a new process permits the manufacture of aluminum with half as much energy as now required, a tremendous saving will have been achieved.

But what is the long term effect of such savings? Reduced prices should reflect lower costs to the manufacturers, part lower energy costs and part lower labor costs. But in a money sense, the savings are all labor costs, because the cost of energy is primarily the costs of labor to extract it and to build all the equipment to do so. The net effect, then, of reduced prices would give the benefit of the saving in energy to the consumer by reducing necessary employment. Since most of us are both consumers and workers, there is a stand-off in net values.

But there is more to the problem. Bruce Hannon points out:

> . . . the finiteness of resources come into view as this nation's striving for a better life spreads internationally. We are beginning to understand the links among heavy consumption, environmental damage, and degradation of the quality of life. We are beginning to see the need for one more adaptive act of humankind, the need for a group morality.

> It should be within the reach of each individual consumer to perceive that he must forgo certain forms of energy consumption now in order to ensure their availability to his offspring or to his own generation in the future. As the human body eventually reaches a condition of zero growth, then so must the population as a whole.[2]

If energy is saved by the individual, he spends less and therefore has income to spend on other things, which also require energy to some degree. Eliminating wasteful use of energy does not in itself solve our problem, if it merely releases funds to be used in other energy-using activities.

In the last analysis, we can reduce energy consumption only by making energy very expensive or by having less income. When activities become more labor-intensive, as they must, lower skills are needed than when the laborer uses extensive energy to increase his effectiveness. With less energy at his command, each hour of work will command lower wages.

Since the highly organized unions have the most people holding high-paying energy-using jobs, they will naturally be opposed to any trend that will increase the number of low paying jobs and decrease those on the higher scale, no matter how necessary it may become. The unions will find it particularly difficult to adapt to an energy-scarce world, particularly as they will be convinced that they are being discriminated against.

If the laws of supply and demand push up the price of energy too fast, all of us will have difficulty changing our lifestyle rapidly to adjust to the new high prices. The impact on lower-income people will be disproportionately high. We are seeing today how agonizingly difficult it is to work out an effective and fair energy policy.

Elimination of energy waste will reduce our per capita energy requirements. Since our U.S. population will continue to climb for many years, however, it will be difficult to bring about a real downturn in total energy consumed. But that is what we must do, whether it is easy or not. The continuing increase in our population inevitably magnifies and intensifies our problem; if our population were ever to decline, the problem would become easy or disappear entirely.

The very scarcity of energy may help us, however. As our economy necessarily becomes more labor-intensive we should be able gradually to eliminate job philosophy because of the increased need for labor. We can hope that the loss in the individual laborer's average effectiveness, because he uses less fuel energy in his work, will be more than offset by the increase in average effectiveness due to the elimination of work that doesn't really benefit the total economy. *In toto,* then, the standard of living might hold its own and even improve, despite the necessarily reduced level of energy available. Such a change could provide a genuine improvement in productivity for the society as a whole. This is what we must work for.

At this point, it is impossible to guess how much our energy use will have to be reduced. Depending upon the speed with which we divert our research and development resources to learning how to tap the immense power of solar energy, we will eventually be able to provide a secure and permanent basic supply of energy which our world inventory of fossil fuel will need only to supplement. Perhaps we will have economical nuclear-fusion power, but no one now knows. I predict, however, that we will never use the nuclear breeder reactor for commercial power, because we will finally recognize its awesome and almost perpetual danger and abandon it as a viable energy alternative.

Regardless of that decision, it seems clear that we will have substantially to reduce our energy use per capita, at least for the next thirty years. The squeeze will be tight; we had better prepare.

But conservation of energy is only the first step. In terms of the total human problem, we do have a zero-sum situtation. In a world of finite area and limited energy, further increase in human population can only mean less for each individual. Once we accept this, our ultimate hope is that we also recognize that the smaller the population, the higher per-capita benefits may be expected.

In earlier societies, the limited natural resources available to the population sharply limited the permissible human number. Malthusian law prevailed. As the Industrial Revolution developed, advancing technology provided new resources to support much larger populations. In its earlier stages, mechanization called for vast numbers of workers to operate the machines that provided the goods upon which the civilization was built. It took a substantial population to provide a market large enough to justify and support large-scale manufacture.

Technology improved, to support a continually growing population. Increasing automation, however, sharply reduced the number of direct workers required to produce the society's goods. Most of the economies of scale can be achieved today with far fewer workers than fifty years ago. Despite every effort to find jobs, substantial unemployment has become continuous rather than cyclic.

Under the circumstances, many of us have the uncomfortable feeling that our human world is gradually deteriorating. Inflation eats away our economic stability everywhere, although faster in most foreign countries than in the United States. New and serious threats to our environment are disclosed almost weekly, even though we are spending vast sums to reduce the pollution we already experience. The crime rate is increasing rapidly worldwide, evidencing a steady breakdown of institutions and morale. Energy is getting scarce and expensive. In the very last few years, we recognize that there may not be enough food much longer to provide our human population with even its present marginal diet.

Who is to blame? Strident voices from every political and economic direction are quick to identify the culprits, although few agree on what to do. A most obvious target is our very technological improvement. Technology has moved too fast, we are told: it has outstripped our ability to use it intelligently. What else has given us pollution, the nuclear bomb, and the tangle of modern life? Others say that our technology hasn't been good enough; it should have solved all these problems and provided us with an even greater abundance of everything we need.

Blame it on the rich. Since only a tiny fraction of our population think of themselves as rich, even though most Americans lead lives that would clearly be deemed by the vast majority of humanity to be rich lives, it is popular to argue that if we took it away from the rich, there would be enough for all. There would not.

The rich, on the other hand, have largely attained their wealth under the capitalist system, and they are convinced that, if government stopped interfering with its free operation, all of us would be immensely better off. After all, the United States, operating as a capitalist society, had the highest per-capita income of any country in the world, at least until certain Arab countries had the temerity to use capitalistic techniques to enrich their people through their oil.

Blame it on Russia and Communist countries. If they were not a constant threat to the peace, we would not have to spend on our defense establishment immense sums which could be better spent to provide a good life for everyone. The Russians have said that they will bury us, and we have to be sure they can't. What they do to subvert us and harry us seems to show that détente may be merely a meaningless phrase. The Communists, of course, claim we are the aggressor nation, with the greatest military establishment, and that we represent the real danger.

Blame it on the decline in the effectiveness of the work ethic, and the increase of permissiveness in society. We pay a tremendous price in waste and inefficiency for sloppy work, crime, and ripoffs and to carry the dead weight of those who do nothing at all. Look at our welfare load, growing beyond belief. No wonder we can't prosper, when such a large proportion of us are a constant drag on our economy, and perform no useful functions at all.

The list of culprits is almost endless. They reflect the individual concerns and biases of each of us. We look for the fix that will set all things right again and get the nation and the world going. We extrapolate from the past to reassure ourselves that economic trends reverse themselves, that recessions and depressions are followed by booms and prosperity. We are natural optimists and firmly believe that things are bound to get better, that something will turn up, that somebody will find the answer and take care of us.

It seems so obvious to me now, what our basic problem is. It has been spelled out to us for at least a generation, but we have paid no attention. In effect, there has been a conspiracy of silence, which persists today, even while the evidence becomes overwhelming. We have refused to show more than occasional awareness of our problem, and then only with a shrug, as if there were little we could do. Recognition of this problem requires a basic reversal of our moral and religious attitudes about an important aspect of our social life, and we have been unwilling to face it.

The problem, of course, is population. Not only in the underdeveloped world, but in the United States today, we are already grossly overpopulated and the continuing increase in our population is making matters worse at an accelerating rate. This is hard to swallow, but it is clearly true we must recognize it now, if we are to have any hope for the future.

Is our population too big already? That is a crucial question, to which my answer is an unequivocal "yes." There are four basic reasons: 1) the increasing burden of population crowding, 2) the acceleration of costs because of premature exhaustion of accessible resources, 3) the threshold effect in overloading the natural environment, and 4) the diseconomies of scale which, when our organizations get too big, more than offset the economies of scale, making production less and less efficient. Technology, far from being the cause of our problems, has instead made such great improvements that, until recently, it has been able to offset the negative effect of too many people. But, even if technology continues its rapid development, it can no longer keep pace with the deterioration which overpopulation is causing.

Since there is only a limited amount of available energy, it is apparent that any population increase will require a reduction of per capita energy use. Our only hope to increase per-capita energy is to reduce human population. Although prospects of population reduction are remote in time, we must talk about them now.

Is there an optimum level of population? If so, what is the optimum level for the United States? For the earth as a whole? How does the technological level of the society affect the optimum? Few people have asked these question, but more are starting to.[3]

If we understand "optimum" as meaning the minimum level that mankind has any realistic chance of achieving in the foreseeable future (as Barry Commoner does), we arrive at a figure far larger than our present population. If, on the other hand, we seek to determine at what level of world population all humans could "lead the good life" in balance with nature, without destroying the environment or exhausting our natural resources, we will probably arrive at a much lower figure, some fraction of the present world population. One leading thinker in this field has suggested that, if all the economies and diseconomies of scale are taken into acccount, the optimum population of the United States (a relatively uncrowded country compared to much of the Orient) will prove to be no more than 50 million, compared to our present 215 million. [4] My personal appraisal would be a somewhat higher figure, although substantially less than our present population level.

We do not have to know precisely what is the optimum population level in the United States or in the world. All we have to know now is that it need not be the level at which the largest number of people can be supported. Rather it should be the level at which all humans can lead the good life in balance with nature, without destroying the environment or exhausting its natural resources. There can be no clear answer—it must be a partly subjective decision and, therefore, a matter of varying personal opinions. Even if agreement on it were possible, it would change with the composition and nature of human society and with the level of technology.

Each person's determination of an optimum population depends upon his view of human values, and the weight he gives to each. Obviously, we must have food, clothing and shelter enough to survive, as perhaps the only absolute essentials. Beyond that, as Lincoln H. Day has said, we need "serenity, dignity, order, leisure, peace, beauty, elbow-room—even though man can, on occasion, with his extraordinary powers of adaptability, become inured to severe deprivation with respect to one or the other."[5] He quotes Ansley Coale:

"It is my observation that the disadvantages of a larger population are seen most vividly by those who were born in an earlier era. Often the current inhabitants see nothing wrong with many of the changes that older citizens decry. I feel deprived by the disappearance of open land around Princeton. My children never miss it." [6]

I also plead guilty to this particular bias. Human adaptability is both an advantage and a danger, as Day points out:

> This fluid nature of human values would seem, in fact, to constitute a major threat to any effort to block progressive deterioration in the quality of environment. For there is a real tendency to adjust to the debasement of the environment by being willing to settle for less; that is, by lowering our standards of the optimum for human society and individual well being. [7]

We should not lower our human standards, however. Even though any realization of an optimum population is presently impractical, we should think about it. Some fantasy will help. If job philosophy can be eliminated, and work become meaningful as well as rewarding, efficient employment should provide far greater material rewards than we can hope for now, even at much lower levels of fuel energy per capita. If one of the major future incentives in technology development is to conserve resources, save energy, and eliminate waste, we can easily cut in half our consumption without affecting our scale of living. To date, there has been no price incentive to avoid waste, and the result is our unnecessarily energy-intensive society.

If the most important economies of scale can be adequately realized at a population level one half or one quarter our present numbers, we would eliminate the crowding and the hassle of our modern life, without diminishing its amenities. In fact, to the extent that energy and resources are limited, they would be more abundant per capita.

The environment, in particular, would benefit from our smaller numbers. Fifty million people, for instance, instead of the 215 million today, would pollute one-quarter as much. Pollution would still be objectionable, but controlling it for one-quarter of the population would be far less than one-quarter as expensive as it is today, since the quantity of pollution would in many instances drop well below the threshold the ecosystem can handle and absorb naturally.

Picture any American city with about one quarter the present population. Everyone could spread out their apartments and their homes, each having more space, more privacy, and more resources. Traffic congestion would almost disappear. Air and water pollution would become minimal, even without the tremendous investments now planned or being made to alleviate our present environmental problem.

Primogeniture in England was hard on all the children except the eldest son, who inherited the manor house and all the land, but it prevented the fragmentation of estates to the point that individual pieces would be too small to support a family. The younger sons of England's landowners had no choice but to go into the military or diplomatic service or emigrate. There are few such escape hatches today.

In countries where the land is divided equally (and therefore fairly) among the children, the plots of land become so small that no one can make out well. The obviously just decision to distribute one's land equally among one's children often means that none of them will have enough to sustain a decent life. Short term kindness leads to long term cruelty.

If population could eventually diminish and be held near some presumably optimum level, there would be no need for devices such as primogeniture to prevent excessive fragmentation of tangible wealth. In fact, there should be enough for all.

Optimum population is no more than a distant vision today. It is a concept we may not be ready for. A few people have seen this vision, however, and organizations like Negative Population Growth are making first efforts to awaken us to its undoubted possibilities.

Resources are not a fixed quantity. Some will eventually run out, but technology will actualize new resources that may substitute for the exhausted ones and even expand the possibilities of humankind.

Only in a partial sense, is a steady-state society a zero-sum game. If we think of it as a balance between resources and population, to the extent the population is reduced, resources per capita climb. Every improvement in technology, however, changes the available total figure, so that life can improve substantially even if population declines slowly or not at all.

It is in this context that the idea of optimum population may have meaning. It is obvious that the world would do better with far fewer people. The slogan, "The greatest good of the greatest number," can easily be misinterpreted. The "greatest number" really means "the highest possible percentage of the total." It was never a plea for a bigger population.

A steady-state society at a supposed optimum population level need not be thought of as a utopia. Utopias which are supposedly "ideal human societies," are also static. No human institution can or should stay unchanged for long.

The concept of optimum population is valuable once we let our minds picture an uncrowded world in which the abundant resources we command are not divided among too many people. Science fiction writers have seen this well. Their constructs of future and presumably superior societies invariably have small and uncrowded populations.[8] Philosophers like Plato and Thomas More clearly recognized the dangers of overpopulation.

A few of us have the personal perspective of well over half a century. I remember well what this country was like in the nineteen twenties, in both the big cities and the small towns, from coast to coast. It was a different world largely because there were half as many people in it as there are today. In fact, by comparison with the present, it seemed as if there were less than half as many people. I believe that this was so because the average income was then so low that most people seldom strayed from the narrow path between work and home and, therefore, were rarely seen in the public places which teem with the comings and goings of even the poorest people today. In view of our increase in average income, in a future possible world, an even smaller population than half a century ago might be too many.

Excessive population can be shown to be at the root of most of our problem already. Although there is still room on the earth's surface for billions more people and, with full employment of available technology, we could feed, clothe, and shelter them all, why should we assume that we have no other direction to take?

ŕ) The disadvantages of the physical crowding we already endure, even in the United States, are obvious, once we think about them. True, we have exacerbated them by cramming ourselves into urban areas, but there are some sound economic reasons for this. We endure air pollution, traffic congestion, crowded community areas, inferior housing, a high crime environment, and the anonymity of the big city because it pays us. To a major extent, these are costs of excessive population, which can be only at disproportionate expense, particularly so long as our population continues to rise.

2) I have discussed the diseconomies of scale, first as applied to business and industry, but then as they affect our whole society. These diseconomies are not directly proportional to size: they rise much, much faster. We feel their pressure today, although we tend to attach other labels. Just one example: the incidence and severity of floods along our rivers will continue to increase as long as we pave over more and more of our country and put up more and more housing developments on land that used to absorb the rain and delay runoffs. The costs of raising higher dikes to hold back the water and prevent the damage the floods still cause are clearly costs of too many people. Look around you and you will find many other examples.

3) Our present population already endangers the total natural ecosystem of which we are an integral part. Ever since man evolved from his primate ancestors, he has had a major effect on his environment. As primitive hunter, he killed off many animal species which could not compete with his developing skills. As farmer and herdsman, he overfarmed and overgrazed millions of acres, making deserts and barren lands out of fertile areas. Population pressures have required massive destruction of forests partly by clearing for farmland and partly to supply building material fuel and as a raw material for processed chemicals.

The damage we are now doing, however, is on a vastly greater scale, and threatens not only animal and plant life on the land, but the life relationships in the oceans upon which the whole environmental system depends. With a smaller population, even within a highly technological society, most of our impact on the environment would not reach the thresholds that mark the limits of abuse the system can stand and recover from.

4) The depletion of all kinds of natural resources is accelerated by excessive population. Mines have to be dug deeper; poorer-grade ores have to be used. The extra expense of offshore drilling for oil, first in the Gulf of Mexico and now in the North Sea would not have been necessary despite high per-capita consumption, except for there being so many of us. The development of the oil resources of the Alaska North Slope at tremendous expense and at considerable environmental cost is necessary only because too many of us used up too fast our vast oil reserves in the continental United States.

5) Everything costs more when our population numbers climb. Much of our human effort goes for the capital expenses of building commercial and industrial structures, new houses, new roads, and new equipment to cope with more people. Costs climb faster than population because, as space becomes more valuable, it must be used more intensively and extensively. Our technology has improved just fast enough to give us the illusion that we are keeping up. We are *not*.

6) Perhaps most insidious of all, is the loss of individual freedom that is inevitable in a crowded world. Even so simple a freedom as driving an automobile is becoming more and more circumscribed. Stoplights proliferate as traffic increases. Our interstate highways have made long-distance driving tolerable, with tremendous benefit to the trucking industry, but local travel is only worsening. In *Population Vs. Liberty*,[9] Jack Parsons shows graphically how many of our liberties have been limited by our numbers. We all know the puzzle in which there

are fifteen numbered pieces to be slid around in an enclosed board with sixteen spaces. The goal is to arrange them in numerical sequence, and it is not easy. Our traffic situation is already almost that bad.

Under any system of law we relinquish many freedoms, from the freedom to kill another human being to the freedom to run through a stoplight. We live with thousands of these restrictions every day. In a sparsely populated land, few restraints on our freedom were necessary, because our lives and rights infringed only occasionally on those of others.

Garrett Hardin has emphasized that, in our increasingly populous world, not only are our freedoms more limited, but even participatory democracy becomes almost impossible.

> With population increase, . . . (i)ncreasingly complex hierarchies must be devised. The individual must emotionally accept his personal political impotence . . . Every increase in population size requires the renunciation of a larger proportion of the democratic ideal.[10]

We are there already, and we are adjusting little by little to becoming anonymous punchcards in a system that runs by itself, largely out of control.

I am not suggesting that there is much that we can do in the short range about excessive population. The subject is discussed at length here because we need an awakening awareness of the damage we are doing to ourselves and our world by human overpopulation, present and future. Until this awareness becomes widespread and general, warnings of pending disaster will go unheeded.

Some doomsayers suggest that the population problem will

be solved for us when an almost inevitable catastrophe (not necessarily nuclear) devastates the earth within no more than half a century and cuts down our world population by half or three-quarters in one giant calamity. Let us hope that there is a less traumatic road to a stabler world.

If we see the full dimensions of our problem, we will be more willing to make the necessary sacrifices and adjustments to solve it. The imaginative use of a new capitalism to maximize our strengths seems both desirable and possible.

Capitalism need not be incompatible with a steady-state society, even if we eventually control our human population not just to stop its growth, but to bring it down to a saner level. If we can show sufficient restraint in breeding children, all else becomes possible. Capitalism can not only survive but thrive in a no-growth world to the benefit of us all.

Why is the capitalistic system still appropriate, although with some changes? The protagonists for socialism and all its modifications and variations have argued that only through socialism can the best results be obtained. Historically, however, they have been almost 100% wrong, because again and again free enterprise capitalism has provided more material benefits to a wider spectrum of the population than any other system. In fact, without the benefits of the efficiency of the capitalistic system, our material standard of living would probably suffer a serious decline.

No other system has shown that it can provide as high a material standard of living. Without the capitalist system, we can *all* expect to be much poorer. Retaining capitalism in a steady-state world, therefore, is a necessity if we are to avoid deterioration of an economy below the level we would be willing to tolerate.

Can Capitalism Survive?

Providing the material necessities of life for our vast population requires the immensely efficient technological organization of our economic society. If we are to continue to feed, clothe and shelter us all and to provide the amenities we have come to expect, the economic system must continue to function smoothly.

What are its strengths, which make it worth keeping? I believe that its principal strengths are two: 1) its powerful incentives to individual effort and 2) the market mechanism that provides the correcting feedbacks which help to keep the system in balance.

What makes Sammy run? What are the incentives that capitalism uses so well to make our economy improve? The desires for money (profits), the better life, power, recognition, personal fulfillment, and the feeling of accomplishment. Growth has been an effective means to fulfill these desires, but it is not a goal in itself. Somehow, we must design ways other than growth to fuel the capitalist engine.

Money is only one measure of success. In a no-growth society, money would have to defer to other devices, such as title, responsibility, authority, perquisites, amenities, special privileges, prizes, prestige, and publicity. Used with appropriate skill and restraint, no one can doubt that these other devices are effective.

Growth of enterprises to great size today, regardless of the obvious diseconomies of scale, makes one wonder whether the search for power for its own sake is not a crucial component in the desire for growth. Are there other satisfactions that can take the place of the thrill of corporate power? Why do people seek national public office? "Serving the people" is a useful euphemism for satisfying one's egoistic needs.

Can Capitalism Survive?

I believe that incentives can be developed for a slow-growth or no-growth society sufficient to provide much, if not all, of the benefit of capitalistic free enterprise in an expanding economy. We must go back to our needs as defined by Douglas McGregor. Obviously, there are satisfactions that can substitute for money and power, and we will do well to find and use them.

Although capitalism is supposed to make its principal appeal to the material side of our nature, the analysis of our different needs shows that that is too narrow a view. Capitalism and greed are not necessarily synonymous, nor is man necessarily acquisitive by nature. Anthropologists can show us a number of societies in which altruism seems to function effectively in the group interest, and others where possession of goods is unimportant. Somehow we must tap these other powerful motivations.

How about the market mechanism of capitalism? There is tremendous virtue in the free working of the law of supply and demand. I see no reason why this needs major modification. I have always been in favor of strict enforcement of anti-trust legislation (even though, like most businessmen, I have sometimes found myself secretly wishing that my chief competitor would raise his prices so that I could too). Competition is essential for the proper functioning of the market mechanism.

My personal experience has been that competition is very real. Our business might be the sole producer of left handed anodized aluminum 3″ widgets and, therefore, have a theoretical monopoly of a particular tiny market. In practice, however, the purchaser can usually find an adequate substitute and will buy our product only if the quality and service are good and the price not too unreasonable. When consumers have acquired the necessities of life and are selecting how they will spend their discretionary dollar, the washing machine manufacturer is competing directly with the travel agent and the curtainmaker.

The market mechanism will work differently in the future world, in that competition in specific products and services will be more localized. But competition can still be effective enough to prevent monopolistic practices.

In the early years of our country's history, our infant industries needed protective tariffs in order to survive and grow in competition with imports. Today our American industry is so powerful, and our multinational companies so strong, that we effectively deter the growth of native industries in much of the developing world. They can't compete with us.

All my life, in viewing the world economy, I have argued for unrestrained free trade. I believed that each country should do what it does best and that consumers everywhere would be wisest to buy from the best and most efficient producer, wherever it is located. I assumed unlimited economies of scale, and discounted the costs of transportation and distribution.

A developing country may be better off, however, to support its native industry by imposing protective tariffs on the imported goods, even though it means its citizens pay higher prices for the things they need.

Providing useful employment to its own people is more important to its economy than insuring that its citizens have the advantage of the very lowest cost. What good is it to have low prices if no one has the ability to buy at any price? The developing countries, in particular, need to be protectionist at least until they are fully ready to compete with more industrialized countries on their own terms.[11]

Free trade encourages specialization, but at the cost of self-sufficiency. As higher energy costs make transportation of goods more expensive, and as we move toward a more labor-intensive world, the importance of self-sufficiency increases. Even without protective tariffs, in the future, local industry will be able to compete more effectively with the world's most efficient producers through having lower transportation and distribution costs. The level of activity above which the dis-economies outweigh the economies of scale will be much lower. Smallness will come into its own, both in business and in community size.

If capitalism is to survive and thrive, it will have to adapt to a different world. Our most difficult and painful task will be to achieve more equality of wealth without destroying the incentives of capitalism. Greater distributive justice is absolutely necessary, however.

In simpler words, that means that wealth must be spread more evenly than it is today. The extreme disparities in income and wealth of our present society are the result of cancerous growth. I doubt that the major adjustments that our economy will face can be made peacefully unless everyone shares in the cost.

What is the purpose of wealth in an economy in which there is enough for all to have the necessities of life, plus some incre-ment of "luxuries"? In ancient societies, such as the Greek and Roman civilizations, one justification of differential distribu-tion of goods was that an élite was necessary to create and transmit the culture that made man better than animal. The masses slaved so that the few could have the leisures necessary to hold the civilization together.

Today, our slaves are largely mechanical, so we need a different rationale. (It has been calculated that, in the United

States, we have the equivalent of three hundred slaves each). Capitalism provides the necessary incentives for the hard work and risk-taking essential to success. The reward is wealth (and power). To the extent that society benefits from the efforts so motivated, wealth is justified. But how much wealth?

Plato proposed that the difference in the stock of wealth of the richest and the poorest citizens should be in a ratio no greater than four to one (4:1). Since in our civilization the poorest citizens have no wealth at all, any ratio today seems meaningless. But, even eliminating from our calculations the very poorest and the very richest among us, the difference in wealth must be more on the order of 1,000:1 today.

Although a 4-to-1 differential seems far too low, our present range from top to bottom is too great. Successful capitalism need not require such extravagant rewards to insure adequate motivations. Some of this differential may disappear naturally, as the economic changes I foresee turn us to smaller activities, not only in industry, trading areas and community size, but in opportunities for making individual giant fortunes.

I am not an egalitarian; I do not want to see everyone brought to the same level. If we are all made fully equal, while some individuals may benefit temporarily, the society as a whole can only suffer.

> . . . freedom and equality are sworn and everlasting enemies, and when one prevails the other dies. Leave man free and their natural inequalities will multiply almost geometrically . . . To check the growth of inequality, liberty must be sacrificed . . . Even when repressed, inequality grows . . . in the end superior ability has its way. Utopias of equality are biologically doomed.[12]

We will require the precise balance between equality and freedom that will maximize the strengths of the civilization while distributing its benefits as widely as possible. Balancing the rights to equality and freedom requires major compromises by both capitalists and egalitarians to achieve the healthiest total society.

I do not know what the maximum differential of wealth between rich and poor should be, except that it ought to be substantially smaller than it is today. As one step, our estate and inheritance tax system should be strengthened to tax unrealized capital gains at death and to include gifts made before death. Next we need to place some restrictions on the amounts that may be passed on by inheritance. This is a major subject in itself, which has no obvious or easy answer. If capitalism is to succeed in a steady-state society, however, we must act.

In a world of smaller communities, both social and economic, the reduction of great disparities in personal wealth will be easier. It is important that the wealthy become a more integral part of their local communities, rather than escape to isolated enclaves where they communicate only with their financial peers. Although many of the wealthy are actively involved in community matters, many others shun any contact with the hoi polloi and instead find a shelter to hide in to avoid contamination by life.

Capitalism has an image of selfishness. Its motivations are rooted in individual self interest. But if successful realization of our individual self interest depends primarily on the welfare of the whole, as it does in our closely-knit society today, the capitalist will need a broader view of his role in the economy. Gerard Piel puts it thus:

> In the civilization of high technology, no man can improve his lot at the expense of others; what diminishes them must, sooner rather than later, diminish him.[13]

Kenneth E. Boulding speaks of

> [The] "invisible college" of people . . . who have this vision of the nature of the transition through which we are passing and who are determined to devote their lives to contributing toward its fulfillment.[14]

That "invisible college" must be expanded to include a majority of us.

It is my hope that when we begin to understand the long range general interest, most of us will discover that it is our own and our family's long term personal interest, too. Standard capitalistic motivations assume that pursuing individual ends best assures the welfare of the economy as a whole. I am suggesting that, in the future, self-interest may best be served by pursuing public goals.

Smallness is important to achieving effective altruism. Mankind evolved as a species in small groups, each one largely isolated from all others. Those individual traits survived which best helped the group as a whole to survive. J.B.S. Haldane, the eminent biologist, once showed mathmetically that the biological advantage of individual altruistic conduct has evolutionary survival value only if a substantial proportion of the group act altruistically.[15]

Elsewhere, the Nobel Prize-winning geneticist Hermann J. Muller has noted:

> (The) predisposition to be of service to others of the immediate family will be of selective advantage . . . the larger the community to which he extends such help . . . the weaker [the selective advantage]. Selection for altruistic properties has tended to work chiefly for those traits that cause help to be given very near at home.[16]

What does this mean? If a single person in a very small group acts in the group interest, even though it harms him personally, the group will be better off and the chances of group survival will be benefited more than the unselfish act will hurt the individual. A certain amount of unselfishness has been bred into us because we evolved in small isolated groups.

In large groups, however, the individual's action has little influence. In our immense and largely anonymous modern society we all come to feel that what we do individually does not matter to the community or nation as a whole. As a result, we have become more accustomed to putting Number One first, to the point that this is now acceptable behavior in many circles.

The people who respond to a call for help by saying, "I don't want to get involved," have learned that they will not be callled to account, because they can step away into the relative obscurity of the anonymous crowd. Petty theft and shoplifting may have gained impetus from the impersonality of the giant corporation, which is presumed to be too big to feel or care about the loss one individual causes.

If each of us is an immeasurably small part of the whole, it scarcely matters what any one of us does. We react accordingly.

William Ophuls has put it:

> . . . it is precisely the essence of the tragedy of the commons that one's own contribution to the problem seems so infinitesi-

mally small, while the disadvantages of self-denial loom very large. Whenever one's real interests are engaged, self-restraint appears to be both unprofitable and ultimately futile unless one can be certain of universal compliance.[17]

Many of our laws are based on an implicit recognition that most people will obey them without question. Enforcement of the income tax laws, for example, depends for its effectiveness on the voluntary compliance of almost all citizens. Most of us report honestly, even when we know the chances of being penalized for omissions or mistakes, honest or not, are small. Our society depends on the basic goodness of most people. This reservoir of integrity will be tremendously important in adjusting to our future world.

If we are to make a successful transition to a different kind of economy, we will need the willingness of a substantial proportion of our people to put the general interest ahead of their own personal interest in many ways. In a totally interwoven world economy where each person is an infinitesimal part of the whole, we tend to lose the very qualities we will need for survival. In a world divided into many more or less self sufficient regions or communities, however, individual sacrifices will have greater impact and, therefore, are more likely to be made.

In a small business, the community of interest among the members of the organization tends to be closer and decisions tend to be made for the benefit of the business, rather than for the sole benefit of one individual. In a small community, where interpersonal communications are good, there is more awareness of what is for the general benefit and greater willingness to make personal sacrifices to forward general purposes.

Since it is important to each of us that we all pull together to support the general welfare, we should welcome any means of structuring our society to strengthen the cohesive forces of community that will best encourage such conduct. Smaller is indeed better—in business and in personal life. Have we not had enough of the indifference and anonymity of the mass society? We will do better to work our way back to the closer and more rewarding ties of the smaller world.

Capitalism can succeed in a no-growth society with some help from all of us:

1   A necessary individual concern for the general interest can best be stimulated by thinking small, that is, by moving toward a world of smaller communities and smaller businesses. Eventually, we will want to work toward a smaller or "optimum" total human population.

2   A reduction in total consumption of energy seems inevitable. If job philosophy and waste can be drastically reduced, more or less simultaneously, however, that might mean only a minor reduction in the quality of the life we can lead or perhaps none at all.

3   A careful reduction in the extremes of wealth and poverty will be needed to achieve as much "distributive justice" as will be compatible with maintaining the effectiveness of capitalist incentives.

If capitalism is thus modified, is it still capitalism or, in the transition, has it become something else? If today's economic

system can still properly be defined as capitalism, the changes I
see as inevitable will not alter it much more than it has already
been modified.

The equity in the corporation will still be owned by its
shareholders, although new restrictions will be added to those
we already endure. Limitations on wealth and income will be
more severe, but not different in basic thrust from the progressive taxation we are now used to. Job philosophy will not be
eliminated by any government attempt to legislate what should
or should not be done but by solving chronic unemployment
problems by other means. The market mechanism will continue
to function, except that industry will be expected to absorb the
costs of polluting the environment which it has largely passed
on to the public in the past. Necessarily we will give more
weight to preserving our environment for the benefit of future
generations, and will structure our incentives to insure this.

What are the trends we may expect?

1   The diseconomies of scale will become more sig-
    nificant and more obvious, thus encouraging reduc-
    tions in the scale of operations.
2   As transportation costs increase because of higher
    energy prices, different regions will become economi-
    cally more independent. Local manufacture and dis-
    tribution will tend to supersede national and interna-
    tional marketing.
3   The economy will become more labor-intensive and
    less energy-intensive, thus accelerating the above
    trends.
4   If the tax laws are modified so that they no longer

encourage growth and large size, the push will be in
the same direction toward smallness.

5 In a smaller society, job philosophy will be easier to
recognize and its reduction will be more obviously
necessary and, therefore, easier to achieve.

If we can make these adjustments gradually, we can maintain
a vigorous and free society in which individual opportunity can
be as great as ever. But it will be a different and more difficult
kind of opportunity. Growth is a much easier strategy, because
it tends to bury its own mistakes. As long as everything grows,
we all have the illusion of success, even when we fall behind in
relation to others.

Growth's companion, inflation, provides this illusion. When
the union extracts a wage increase from the employer, the
wage-earner feels that his income has increased, even when
continuing inflation whittles it away.

In the long run, the laborers who make a product cannot
justify receiving more than a limited percentage of the sales
price. Most of the sale price must inevitably go to purchase the
material and supplies, provide the work place and the tools and
equipment, promote the sales and advertising effort to move the
goods, pay for the administrative work necessary to control the
enterprise, and make enough profit to attract the funds necessary to do all these things.

When the laborer negotiates too large a share, for more than a
short time, others must get too little. The owners who supply
the funds are at the end of the line. If their share is cut too far,
new money cannot be attracted and the business cannot survive.
Eventually, the underpaid owners sell or abandon the business
and look elsewhere for adequate rewards.

The average wage-earner doesn't understand this, however. He believes that corporate profits are immense—a bottomless well available to the shrewd bargainer. If the union leaders know that isn't true, they rarely say so. Inflation rescues them from the admission that there is no more to be had. "I got you an increase, didn't I? I can't help it if inflation gradually eats it up."

In a no-growth economy, there are no such easy answers. Spades must be called spades. All leaders, business, labor, and political, will be faced with pressures that cannot be dodged. Gurney Breckenfeld puts it:

" . . . a low-growth economy will reward wisdom instead of aggressiveness. It will put a premium on prudence, efficiency and cost-cutting.[18]

Not very inspiring virtues, perhaps, but we must be ready to praise and encourage them.

All this will place the ultimate responsibility on the individual, at all levels. If, as I believe, the present decline in sense of responsibility is in large part a disease of bigness, there is a cure, albeit a slow one.

As we are pushed toward smallness, we will become more sensitive to the needs and pressures of our immediate world. The sense of community, so diluted today, will flower again. Our young people have reacted adversely to the bigness and impersonality of our society. Unwittingly, we may have prepared them for the world to come better than we realized.

Most of us who believe in capitalism have great difficulty in facing up to this problem at all. Unless we do, however, there is little hope that a smooth adjustment can be made. We find it easier to deny that growth need come to an end, at least for a long time.

It is not a consciously ostrichlike attitude. If we carefully select the input of information we rely upon, we can convince ourselves that there is no foreseeable end to growth. The editor of *The Economist*, a publication highly regarded both in Britain and the United States, considers as red herrings the widely held beliefs that growth will be stopped by shortages of 1) energy, 2) food, 3) raw materials, or the effects of 4) pollution, and 5) high birth rates.[19]

If you are convinced that capitalism depends upon growth for survival, you can hardly admit that growth will have to end. I like growth, too; it makes life much easier. But I am convinced that we have no choice. I only hope we can make the best of the difficult situation we face.

The argument to think small is not a suppressed desire to climb back into the womb or a nostalgia for the olden days. Nor is it a manifestation of a determination to punish success and all those who are economically successful; I am not a masochist.

There is real question whether a vibrant capitalism can survive in a steady-state society. I only say that it has a chance and that it is worth all the thought and effort we can muster to give it a good try. If the businessmen fight every adjustment to the end, they will be disfranchised and effectively disemboweled. If government attempts to fill the vacuum when the free market system is destroyed, everyone will suffer from economic ineptitude, bureaucracy and oppression. *1984* will indeed have arrived.

8

Design for Survival

WHAT IS OUR COLLECTIVE RESPONSIBILITY AS HUMAN BE-INGS? Are we responsible only for ourselves? For our immediate family? For our community? Our country? All living humans? All life on our planet? At different times, in different ways, we may think of all of these. What about responsibility for the future? For our children's children and their children and so on? For the future of mankind? For the future of life itself?

If each of us cares only about his own personal skin, it is possible to survive unscathed for the rest of one person's lifetime, regardless of what happens to others. If we go so far as to be concerned about our children's lives, however, total selfishness won't work, because we won't be there to protect them and money alone will not suffice to shield them from drastic change.

When human population was relatively small, we did not have to be concerned about the total ecological system in which we were still a minor and uninfluential part. When civilization began, however, so did our serious impact on the system. The deserts of the Middle East are an early witness to our careless power: we made them. In this century our burgeoning technology has permitted an immense expansion of our population which has thereby become the dominant factor in our world life-system. Unknowing, and often uncaring, we disrupt and destroy stable and complex ecological balances that took millions of years to evolve.

I do not argue that Nature is always right. Some changes man has made, such as turning the dark, impenetrable forest we found in eastern America into the varied countryside of a generation ago, must be an improvement not only for mankind, but for hosts of species of plant and animal life. But now we are suppressing Nature, not just altering it, largely because there are so many of us that, in order to satisfy our immediate needs, our day-to-day survival requires extermination of whatever is in our way.

If any other species were to become as extensive and powerful as man, the balance would be destroyed and the ecological system would eventually collapse bringing down that species with it. Marston Bates once pointed out

> . . . that the more complex the biological community the more stable [it is] . . . The intricate checks and balances among the different populations in a forest or sea look inefficient and hampering from the point of view of any particular population, but they insure the stability and continuity of the system as a whole and thus, however indirectly, contribute to the survival of particular populations.[1]

Destruction by man has simplified the ecosystem in the name of efficiency. It is a dangerous course.

Design for Survival

We are responsible for the entire ecological system. We cannot endure without it, and if we fail to protect it, man will join the dinosaurs in extinction. So will a multitude of other species. We don't have to protect all life; unlike the Hindus who believe that all life is sacred, we need not stop swatting flies. The individual of any species is important only if its death endangers the perpetuation of the total system. Our concern must be with each species as a whole, as it relates to all others. Each species we eliminate changes the equilibrium of the whole ecosystem; we had better know just what we are doing.

If, as individuals, we care only about our present generation (ourselves, our children and perhaps our community) we can probably survive for another ten or twenty years with minimum adjustments to the tightening squeeze. We can ignore the all-too-frequent signs that we are running into a cul-de-sac. But a substantial number of us would be well-advised to look ahead.

We are fortunate that many are deeply concerned about the irreversible changes in our world made by the sweep of a careless hand. Organizations like The Nature Conservancy are dedicated to saving the last unspoiled areas of our land before we destroy them. Other groups like The Friends of the Earth battle to save us from shortsighted legislation which creates long-range problems. Most basic, however, are those who attack head-on the problem of our human numbers. Unless our population (both here and around the world) can stop growing and eventually shrink, all is lost.

In the matter of population, for instance, if too many couples in the next decades have large families (a common and proper individual goal a generation or so ago), the resulting excess of population will make the "good life" impossible for everyone and bring us all to catastrophe. Since it is impossible to achieve all our individual goals simultaneously, we will need to know which goals must have priority.

Take a relatively simple decision such as the purchase of a new automobile. Most of us need to buy a new car every few years. What are the factors that should influence our decision? We have to evaluate and work out for ourselves the tradeoffs involved, and this is hard to do until we examine our long range goals and purposes.

So long as only the affluent owned automobiles, there was no need to consider the complex interrelationships of automobile ownership with the total environment. It was enough that more people could drive bigger cars faster and farther. Now, as a people, we are beginning to realize that we overlooked some important considerations in our rush to lead the fuller life.

The purchase of an automobile is now more than a personal (or family) decision. All citizens have an interest in your choice. How much irreplaceable fuel energy will you use? How much will you pollute? Should you pay a penalty (presumably in taxes) for buying an excessively big car which wastes fuel? What is each person's responsibility to all his fellow citizens? When our special self interest conflicts with the general public interest, how do we reconcile them?

"Let the future take care of itself" is perfectly good advice if, by future you mean a hundred thousand years hence. But if you mean later this week, it probably is not. How far ahead should we look? Discounting future values monetarily works out so as to give little weight to what happens twenty years from now. But twenty years is within the lifetime of the overwhelming majority of those now living, not to mention those yet unborn.

Personally I am concerned about my life, my children's life, and that of my grandchildren. I am unable to look farther ahead. Because I am worried about my immediate descendants I have to worry about mankind as a whole, for their futures are inseparable. Whatever drastic is going to happen, in my opinion, will happen no later than fifty years from now.

Monetary theory may not place much value on what is fifty (or even twenty) years away, but I do. Many students of the future fear an earlier collapse with incalculable effects. The system is beginning to fall apart, as daily we impose more strains on it. How long can it last? No one knows.

Meanwhile our politicians run around making temporary fixes. None of them is willing to face what the problem really is. Many of our leaders are well read and intelligent, but they don't dare think the unthinkable, because it is political suicide. Of necessity, they are puppets of public impulse. As Roger Revelle said bitterly, "For the politician in a democratic society, infinity is the election after the next one."[2] Until the general public is educated to look beyond its collective nose, no more can be expected of a democracy.

Any manager who has negotiated a labor contract can be sympathetic with the politician. If your business faces a strike that will be catastrophic in its immediate consequences, you may temporize by giving future increases or by making management concessions which, after all, won't be painful until next year or the year after. If you face a tough bargainer, you are tempted to pay any future price to avoid present calamity. In the same way, every politician knows that he can consider long-term issues only when he is sure of winning the next election.

Even when we ignore short-term political consequences, it is difficult to plan ahead in an increasingly complex and interlocked world. The choices we make have consequences that are usually far from obvious. Short-term fixes are likely to have exactly reverse longer-term effects. Jay Forrester has written: "With a high degree of confidence we can say that the intuitive solutions to the problems of complex social systems will be wrong most of the time."[3]

What kind of life does each of us want? We tend to assume the goals without analyzing them. When Samuel Gompers was asked what he wanted in a labor contract for his union, he said "More!" Many would make the same answer about our personal or business economic goals. That is no longer a good answer, but it is not always easy to see why.

We cannot think too simplistically. As one example, the humanitarianism that is one of the best expressions of man's nature is being torn apart by the recognition that short-term kindness is often long-run cruelty. Does that mean that we can no longer be kind, but must become callous to today's misery in order to avoid even worse tragedy for a few years ahead? To quote A. V. Hill:

> The dilemma is this. All the impulses of decent humanity, all the dictates of religion and all the traditions of medicine insist that suffering should be relieved, curable diseases cured, preventable disease prevented. The obligation is regarded as unconditional: it is not permitted to argue that the suffering is due to folly, that the children are not wanted, that the patient's family would be happier if he died. All that may be so; but to accept it as a guide to action would lead to a degradation of standards of humanity by which civilization would be permanently and indefinitely poorer . . .

Some might [take] the purely biological view that if men will breed like rabbits they must be allowed to die like rabbits . . . Most people would still say no. But suppose it were certain that the pressure of increasing population, uncontrolled by disease, would lead not only to widespread exhaustion of the soil and of other capital resources but also to continuing and increasing international tension and disorder, making it hard for civilization itself to survive. Would the majority of humane and reasonable people then change their minds? If ethical principles deny our rights to evil in order that good may come are we justified in doing good when the foreseeable consequence is evil?[4]

Our education does not prepare us for the complexities of our modern world. We are used to simplistic unidirectional reasoning. Before World War II, physics was the dominant science. The purpose of an experiment was to establish conditions in which the phenomenon to be observed could be treated as a single event with a single cause clearly bringing about the single effect without outside interference. Even though this purity of analysis did not reflect conditions in the real world, we came to believe that all problems could be reduced to direct cause-and-effect analysis, provided we broke them down to their basic elements.

Since World War II, biology has become the queen of sciences. Biological systems are incredibly complex. We are learning to recognize that we must look at each system as a whole, because the interactions and feedbacks are too interrelated to be analyzed one by one. (Fortunately, the computer has become available as an essential tool in studying complex systems.) We find that life is a tightly interwoven web, in which simple black and white answers are no longer good enough.

In the less populous and less technological world of a generation ago, a society could survive with simple answers, partly because the consensus was close enough to the truth or, more often, because our society could endure an incredible number of wrong and partly wrong decisions and still prosper. When communities and regions were largely self-sufficient economically, decisions made in one place had little or no effect a hundred or a thousand miles away. Our present technological civilization is so interdependent and interlocked that a variation in climate halfway around the world has immediate and profound effects on American economy.

Today we have to be a great deal smarter. In facing our present problems, we are being forced to look beyond the primary and immediate consequences of what we do. We must have a widespread awareness of the complexity of life and society and their interrelationships.

When one's world starts to go wrong, it is natural to blame a single apparent cause of the problem. The selected devil usually is the most obvious villain and often the closest at hand. We tend to blame the energy crunch on the oil companies just as, a short time ago, housewives picketed the supermarkets because of high beef prices. In the latter case, they didn't know (or didn't care) that per capita beef consumption in the United States had doubled in the last quarter century while the population had grown more than 50% (thus, total consumption had tripled), so that it was amazing that prices had not risen even more.

Many thinking people believe that implacable forces are in the saddle both in this country and throughout the world and that mankind is being helplessly swept along by the very technology which it created. The human world is now so complex and the economic forces and pressures in it interact among each other so rapidly that no individual or group can comprehend a fraction of what is happening. Thus, there is a very real feeling of helplessness and a loss of direction, because the old rules no longer work.

When recalcitrant people or machines disrupt our lives, we look for a scapegoat, some individual who caused it or let it happen. We may also think about finding some person who can impose order on our chaotic world to make things work as they should. That way lies Fascism. But assigning guilt to devils of our choice will not solve our problems, even though the resulting emotional catharsis may make us feel better for a short while. Difficult as it is, we must learn to look deeper.

In a relatively uncrowded world, if each person strives to achieve his own personal goals, so long as those goals are not directly opposed to the individual goals of others, the success of each individual tends to support the prosperity of the whole community. The free enterprise economic system depends upon self-interest to motivate the individual to create material wealth which will benefit others. But in a more crowded society, the consequences of each decision become far more complex, and it is difficult if not impossible for the individual to foresee, let alone take into account, the secondary and tertiary consequences of his acts, including all the so-called side effects—what Garrett Hardin calls the "effects which I hadn't foreseen or don't want to think about."[5]

Everybody is talking about ecology today, while five years ago few people knew what the word meant. We are being awakened to the very real threat that conditions are changing so rapidly that the earth may even become uninhabitable. What was once just a bothersome and sometimes amusing smog in Los Angeles has mushroomed into a thousand threats to our whole existence in the air, on the land and in the waters of the world.

New dangers to our lives and futures seem to appear almost every week. The smoke pouring from the stacks of our industries was the first and most obvious hazard. We are discovering that almost everything we do pollutes the atmosphere in one way or another.

Add water pollution to air pollution. While a generation ago in a less populous world, a running stream would purify contaminated water in a quarter mile or so, now we dump such a vast amount and variety of wastes into our streams that we have overloaded the systems; no longer can they purify themselves. Sewage, industrial wastes of all kinds—detergents, pesticides, mercury, cadmium, oil, in fact, almost every product of our civilization—contaminate our rivers and lakes. Even the oceans are being seriously contaminated, perhaps irreversibly.

We have become painfully environment-conscious, but we are treating this condition as we have learned to treat all problems: break it up into its component parts and attack each part as a separate problem. Thus, we are forcing industry to clean up its smokestacks and stop dumping untreated chemicals into our waters. We are requiring the auto industry to reduce drastically the emission of contaminants from car exhausts. We are banning DDT and PCB and certain other pesticides. In some areas, we have banned phosphate detergents. Leaf- and rubbish-burning in cities and suburbs have been banned for some time (although no one has been bold enough to suggest that we stop having fires in our fireplaces). Desperately, we are running off in all directions, trying to keep our world from deteriorating further.

All this is probably necessary. We are increasingly worried, as we should be. When people are worried or scared, it is a good time to get tough about environmental damage, and it is a good way to awaken us to its seriousness.

Our ecological problems have had a special educational result. For the first time, as a people, we have become aware of how a biological system works: we dimly grasp the complex effects of what we do to our environment. While we have tended to oversimplify both problems and solutions, we are gradually getting smarter and more thorough in our analysis of specifically environmental problems. But we are still wearing blinders in relation to the total picture.

For example, the energy crunch was clearly foreseen by many people, but until the population as a whole personally experienced the deprivation and could speak of it in the present tense, it was impolitic for those who must be reelected by popular vote to become interested in considering more than perfunctorily what should or must be done. Because we are unable to think ahead, we tend to attack symptoms and decide on short-term remedies, some of which merely worsen the long-term situation.

As a people, we are used to simple answers to complex questions and refuse to listen to anything else. Certain leaders, political and industrial, have insisted that the analysis of any subject be summarized for them on a single page, saying that anything that cannot be fully comprehended in that space is not worth considering. Although this may be a healthy device to discourage bureaucratic wordiness, it indicates a superficiality of understanding unsuited to today's complex situation.

In the practice of law, one learns that there are two sides to every case and that there are few, if any, absolute rights and wrongs. So fragile is the necessary balance between different and often conflicting freedoms, that no human society can stay unchanged more than momentarily. The right to free speech sometimes conflicts with the right not to be slandered. The right to freedom from crime conflicts with the rights of persons accused of crime to every possible protection under the Constitution.

All of life needs to be subjected to a constant cost/benefit analysis. The tradeoffs must be evaluated by reasonable people with adequate objectivity. We must always be aware of the claims and interests of others with different perspectives. Very little in this world is clearly black and white. No simple approaches or simple rules are going to make everything come out right. A careful balance must be maintained because all of the right is seldom in only one place. Do we protect the constitutional rights of the accused criminal to the extent of endangering the rights of the citizen to reasonable safety and security? Do we insist on absolute safety under all circumstances to the extent of banning a useful product that has occasional adverse effects on a tiny percentage of users? These questions cannot be answered until the particular facts are known and weighed.

All life involves risks. Failure to act at all is in itself a risk. Freeman J. Dyson has written about "The Hidden Cost of Saying No."[6] His title means that, if we seek total safety by forbidding the adoption of any new idea or product until we are entirely certain it is without risk, we have effectively foreclosed change of any kind.

The present strict regulations about the introduction of new drugs became law as a result of public reaction to the thalidomide tragedy, in which thousands of babies were born badly deformed because of a supposedly harmless sleeping pill. One can recognize the necessity to avoid another such multiple tragedy, while also seeing that the regulations mean virtually no new drugs can be introduced in the foreseeable future.

When government says no to one project, it may effectively discourage future projects. The cost of shutting off future development may, in the long run, far exceed the short run security obtained. We must continually study tradeoffs and make use of cost/benefit ratios if we are to improve our world at all.

Dyson concludes

> . . . that bureaucratic regulation has a killing effect on all creative endeavor. No matter how wisely framed and well intentioned, legal formulations tend to be inflexible. Procedures designed to fit one situation are applied indiscriminately to others. Regulations, whose purpose was to count the cost of saying yes to an unsound project, have the unintended effect of saying no to all projects which do not fit into the bureaucratic machine. Inventive spirits rebel against such rules and leave the leadership of technology to the uninventive. These are the hidden costs of saying no.[7]

We cannot expect to be absolutely safe. Nor can we insist on all our rights. Take a situation very much in point: the exposure of doctors and hospitals to malpractice suits. When a surgeon makes a negligent error during an operation, he may cause irreparable harm to the patient who then has recourse to a suit for malpractice. So long as this right was invoked only in cases of clear and gross negligence, the system seemed to work adequately. Today, however, doctors are being sued for every possible action or failure to act which may have had adverse effects on the patient. Since the slightest error may become a malpractice case, the doctor dares take only the most conservative view of his duty to his patient, lest lack of success in using a possibly risky procedure subject him to suit. He does better to let the patient die without an operation than perform one that has an 80% chance of success, because he cannot afford to be sued by the heirs of the 20% who don't make it.

Attention is now focused on the size and number of judgments in malpractice cases. Juries tend to consider that only insurance companies suffer when gigantic penalties are imposed. But the doctor and hospitals pay the premiums, and as the number and amount of judgments increase the size of premiums escalates. These costs necessarily are passed on to the patients in higher fees and hospital bills. To the extent that government services absorb these costs, they are added to the taxes everyone pays.

The magnitude of the problem has brought it to public attention. There is no easy solution in sight. Had the medical profession started to police its own members adequately some years ago, this might not have become a monster. Instead they have done little to establish standards of practice for their profession and have effectively relinquished their control to the courts and the fallible verdicts of judges and juries.

The legal profession is also at fault, having shown little concern for the manner in which many of its greedier members take advantage of the gullibility and vulnerability of people who have suffered from real or presumed failures of doctors in action.

The insurance companies have been very shortsighted. Instead of fighting each case all the way, they settle most cases before trial by making handsome payments. Although in each individual case they may have paid out less than a jury would have allowed, their attitude has encouraged a vast number of claimants to sue in the hope of a settlement, thus exacerbating the total problem. Since they pass on their costs in premiums plus a percentage, their incentive may be to increase rather than reduce litigation. In the long run, this could be a self-defeating policy, because the resulting excesses may destroy the profession they pretend to protect.

The real problem is that the practice of medicine, like everything in life, requires taking certain risks if it is not to stagnate entirely. No surgery can be performed or medicine administered without risk of injury to the patient. If risk is to be totally avoided, we must revert to incantations, although even the witch doctor could be sued for exorcising the wrong spirits. If a sufficient number of patients demand perfect results from their doctors, the practice of medicine will be effectively destroyed. The only imaginable beneficial effect will be a sharp increase in the death rate so that population increase will stop and start to reverse.

All of life involves rights impinging on rights. The concern about protecting the rights of criminals impinges on the rights of ordinary citizens to be free from the danger of these criminals. If some armed robbers paroled from prison commit more armed robberies, whose rights were protected and whose violated? What is the tradeoff? Even freedom of speech is not an absolute right. Intemperate speech can be slanderous and, if vicious enough, even constitute actionable assault.

Is there an answer? How do you protect the right of the injured individual to obtain reasonable redress from the negligent doctor without opening the right so wide that the average doctor can no longer do his job effectively? The medical profession, the legal profession, the insurance industry, and the public at large will have to cooperate to arrive at a reasonable balance of rights and obligations. I see no other way to avoid tearing ourselves apart.

We must remember that, if any society is to survive as a viable entity, the vast majority of its members must be mindful of the so-called social contract. This is an unspoken agreement that we cannot claim all our "rights," but must instead forgo some of them to keep the social machinery from bogging down in chaos and confusion. The moral restraints that the community places on the individual who wants his own way at the expense of others must, in the long run, continue to be the principal means of controlling aberrant behavior. The law cannot do it alone, although it can provide necessary backup.

What has all this to do with our basic problem? Substitute "capitalism" for "the practice of medicine." Substitute "distributive justice" for "malpractice remedies." We will always need the incentives of capitalism to maintain and improve our material standard of living as a whole. But we cannot live with the vast discrepancies in wealth among members of our society. How do we keep the incentives and yet lessen the material rewards? The first step is to recognize that neither pure unrestricted capitalism nor total egalitarianism is the good answer to the problem.

Those who claim that the economy would boom if all the shackles were removed from capitalism haven't really analyzed the long-run situation. I am partly sympathetic to their position, for one can argue that the economy would have recovered from the Great Depression far sooner had the government not interfered with the laws of supply and demand by massive social legislation in the nineteen-thirties.

We can also be sympathetic with the vast mass of people who are demanding equality in all things. But we must recognize that they do not understand that, if they are successful in eliminating all wealth and class distinctions, everyone will first be brought down to their level and then the whole mass will sink even lower, perhaps to chaos.

Wealth is not just an accumulation of goods. It is a system of production and exchange that relies on trust (credit) among men and institutions. Violent revolutions destroy the system and therefore destroy the wealth instead of redistributing it. [8]

Those few who think that revolution is the only way to right all our wrongs fail to understand that revolution almost always serves only to replace one set of rulers with another (the original revolutionists usually being eliminated in the process).

No system is perfect. There can be no such thing as a perfectly happy society. Charles Galton Darwin writes, ''Happiness does not come from a state, but from a change of state''. [9] Even our muscles function only because they are in a continuous state of tension; they never relax entirely until we are dead.

A biological system gets its strength and stability from a balance of the forces that constitute it. Likewise, the individual human and our society as a whole are both subject to constant pressures from the environment and must maintain a delicate equilibrium among them.

Somehow we must strike a balance between the necessity for adequate capitalist incentives and the claims for distributive justice. We will have to work it out pragmatically over a generation or two. First, we will have to recognize the need to do so.

Capitalism now has many restrictions. Talk to any businessman and he will groan about the endless encroachments on his time and freedom. He is harassed from all sides. Government bureaucrats demand not only all kinds of taxes from him but reams of reports on every phase of his operation. Other bureaucrats tell him to have an affirmative action program for minority employment while making rules that forbid him to ask the questions that will tell him whether he is complying or not. Consumer protection agencies attack his products, packaging, and advertising. Unions, with the backing of government, tell him whom he may employ, when, where, and at what. I could go on for pages.

How many restrictions will the capitalist endure before he gives up and decides the prize is not worth the struggle? Great Britain is a case in point. A recent McKinsey and Company study shows that British chief executives are paid only 44% as much as American chief executives (with total remuneration adjusted to cost of living) and yet pay much higher taxes than in any comparable country. (The effective marginal tax rate for a U.S. top management man is 43%. For his British counterpart it is 83%.)

The rates of pay (after taxes) reflect the prevailing British attitude that business executives aren't really very important to the health of the economy. They may also indicate that British executives have been neither hard working nor smart, and are being paid all they deserve.

What is the cause-and-effect relationship between lack of incentives and the appallingly low efficiency and productivity of the British economy? While outsiders say the British executive is already overpaid for what he does, in view of his short hours, laziness, and lack of ambition, his answer is that with such low pay and high taxes there is no incentive to do better.[10] The British experience may show us the limits below which cash incentives may not be reduced, if the system is to work effectively.

We still want those golden eggs, although we are reluctant to give the goose any credit for laying them. In the future, the monetary rewards of capitalistic success will inevitably decrease. We can hope, however, that we will become more aware that we still need the businessman and, therefore, will harass him less. In that event, a reduction in his cash rewards may seem less painful if we are more obviously thankful for his services. If so, we can hope for dedicated effort even without the prospect of the sometimes extravagant emoluments of today's business tycoon.

The transition to greater equality will have to be gradual, however, because the withdrawal pains will be severe.

Transition from growth to no-growth will not come easily. It may not come peacefully. Growth performs the helpful function of releasing tensions. When there is no possibility of expansion, explosions may be the frustrated answer.

We can only hope that the adjustments may be made in gradual stages, covering a generation or more. I would recommend that the necessary changes be imposed in a series of steps, allowing enough time for each individual to prepare for the new world. When zoning regulations are put into effect for real property, an existing building which does not comply with the new regulations is usually permitted to remain as is, at least until the person who owned it at the time the regulations became effective wants to make changes or the building is sold. This is called a variance for a non-conforming use.

The same policy might apply to necessary changes in distribution of wealth. A tax on inheritance by a spouse, for instance, should not be heavy (unless the survivor is many years the younger of the two), but inheritance by children (and all the more so by grandchildren) above a scheduled maximum should be subject to much heavier levies.

The alternatives to gradual and peaceful change are most unpleasant. Change cannot be avoided by refusing to admit its necessity. Speaking as a capitalist whose oxen will be well gored, I would rather have some control over my destiny than to be dragged willy-nilly into the new world (assuming I am not shot first).

I doubt that my generation can or will adjust easily to any such drastic change as I foresee. But our children and their children will, and quickly. It will be a different world, though not without excitement and promise. It is hard for us to see now how a no-growth world will be able to stimulate and motivate them. But it will.

The next generation will have to make the best of necessity, as mankind always has. This is a different kind of necessity, because it does not mean hardship or poverty, except compared to the life of extravagance and waste that only a few of our present generation could ever afford. It can be a far fuller life than humans as a whole have ever experienced.

We have become wrapped up in our technological abilities. I do not mean that we have too much technology; on the contrary, we need far more. But, because of our success in solving some immense technological problems, we have assumed that we can do anything.

How many times have you heard; "If we can put men on the moon, we can eliminate all poverty . . . we can solve the food problem . . . we can lick cancer," or whatever? That is not a valid comparison. Our space programs were complex mechanical and electronic triumphs, but much simpler to attack and solve than almost any sociological problem you can name.

Our technological abilities are said to have outdistanced our ability to work out the problems of living in a technological society. But we don't seem to realize that technological problems are comparatively quite easy. We think we can solve all problems with equal success. 'T ain't so. The distinction between a physics problem, which can be broken up into solvable units, and a biological-systems problem, which cannot, because every aspect interacts with every other aspect, applies here. We must remember it.

The answer, therefore, is not to stop technology until sociological and political abilities catch up, but to move in two directions: 1) become even more sophisticated in our technology so that we can use it better to tackle the tougher problems, and 2) break down our economic units to smaller entities so that they can be handled more easily.

Technology continues to improve. Computers of the next generation will be particularly helpful in tackling the systems problems we face. Also, once our efforts are directed toward making technology energy-efficient rather than merely labor-saving, we will achieve far higher efficiency in the use of the energy we do have.

A number of trends are converging to make smallness more advantageous than ever. Much of this book has been directed to the better opportunities of smallness as compared to the disadvantages of bigness. My argument will be further reinforced as we experience the gradual shift away from energy-intensive activities, which tend to go with bigness.

"Think small" is not a gospel of despair. Although thinking

small will become a necessity for survival, at the same time it can be a strategy for individual success. It works. Not only does it benefit the individual who can distinguish between accomplishment and mere bigness, it helps us all, now and in the future.

The business community is, in the long pull, the most influential single group in our society. Its leaders must begin to see that no-growth (when it does come) will not necessarily be fatal to their personal aspirations. If enough managers can begin to look for ways to improve their own business without growth, they will be better able to look objectively at the total picture. In that way, they can be catalysts for the necessary changes rather than making a safe transition impossible by continuing blindly each on his own particular road to disaster.

The rules of economic life have changed. So long as we refuse to look at the mounting evidence that the old rules no longer work, we are courting disaster. Fresh thinking is vitally needed. Although many thinkers in the academic world can see some of the problems clearly, they lack the experience, skills, and attitudes to develop practical ways of adjusting our economy to meet changing conditions.

Businessmen can help come up with imaginative solutions to our problems, once they can look farther ahead than next month's sales volume. If they fail to recognize that their stake in our future is great enough to justify dedication to finding basic long-term solutions, when chaos does eventually come, blaming the someone else who should have prevented it will be a futile exercise indeed.

Nor will it just be the big businessman we will look to. Giant businesses have a role, because only big companies can assemble the necessary capital and physical and human resources to tackle large tasks. In many instances, big companies have shown themselves more responsive to broad social goals than has small business. Because of its very size and momentum, big business has to plan farther ahead than small business, because it is not nearly so maneuverable. No large corporation can change much on short notice. Big companies, therefore, have found it necessary to evaluate basic economic currents if they are to be well situated five or ten years in the future.

But the small businessman will have to look ahead too. In the future, as I see it, his role in the total economy will become more important than it is now. He is less a captive of the imperatives of the big company structure and its bureaucracy and therefore more able to bring new insights to our problems. It is no accident that most basic inventions are still made by the individual inventor working alone, even though he does not have the support of the research and development staff and facilities of the giant organizations. New ideas come from individual minds, not from committees.

The small business is more maneuverable, and can adapt to changing conditions faster. Flexibility will be immensely important in the years to come. The willingness to consider new ideas and new approaches will be a particularly valuable asset for any management, large or small.

The signs of change will become clearer each year. We had better get used to looking for them, and recognizing them. If we don't look with fresh eyes, we will be wondering why things are going wrong without understanding why.

Can we make the transition to a different kind of world without tearing civilization to pieces? Robert Heilbroner[11] wonders out loud whether mankind's odyssey through time may not resemble a Greek tragedy, in which the hero moves toward the end he has unwittingly arranged for himself. Are we wiser than the lemmings?

A major purpose of this book has been to try to open our minds to new approaches, so we may free ourselves of clichés of thought which few of us have ever examined critically. Personally, I am optimistic that we will muddle through to a stable society. Once we do, the prospects are for a better life for all of us than we can now envision. Let us not assume, however, that humans will become selfless angels. Rather, they can become smart and rational enough to see that their personal selfish interests are best served by joining to improve the welfare of society as a whole.

We must maintain human values through this period to insure that civilization will continue and the quality of life will benefit. I believe that, in thinking of the future, we must remember that, without a deep concern for individual freedom and rights, we will be less than human. At the same time, we must be hard-headed in discarding sentimental palliatives which only make long-term solutions more difficult. Broad education, keen intelligence, and immense goodwill will be more necessary than ever in the decades to come.

I do not believe there are any easy answers. But so far we have not even asked the questions. Time is running out. We had better start.

Notes

CHAPTER 1   *It's a Small World*

1. Dennis L. Meadows et al., *The Limits to Growth* (New York: Universe Books, 1972).
2. Mihajlo Mesarovic and Eduard Pestel, *Mankind at the Turning Point* (New York: E.P. Dutton & Co., Inc., 1974).
3. Wilson Clark, *Energy for Survival* (Garden City, N.Y.: Doubleday & Company, Inc., 1974), p. 56.
4. Georg Borgstrom, *The Food and People Dilemma* (North Scituate, Mass.: Duxbury Press, 1973), p. 17.
5. Wilfred Beckerman, *Two Cheers for the Affluent Society* (New York: St. Martins Press, 1974.)
6. Warren A. Johnson, personal communication, December 15, 1974.
7. Warren A. Johnson, "Muddling Through to a Steady State," unpublished article.
8. Glenn T. Seaborg, "Opportunities in Today's Energy Milieu," *The Futurist*, February, 1975, p. 24.
9. Lester R. Brown, *In the Human Interest* (New York: W. W. Norton & Co., Inc., 1974).

Notes

CHAPTER 2 *The Disadvantages of Bigness*

1. *Chicago Tribune*, February 23, 1975.
2. Cf. Forrest McDonald, *The Phaeton Ride* (Garden City, N.Y.: Doubleday & Company, Inc., 1974).
3. Peter Drucker, *The Practice of Management* (New York: Harper & Row, 1954), pp. 238–9.
4. Cf. Noël Mostert, *Supership* (New York: Alfred A. Knopf, Inc., 1974).
5. Calculations by John W. Legge.

CHAPTER 3 *The Vulnerability of Size*

1. Roberto Vacca, *The Coming Dark Age* (Garden City, N.Y.: Doubleday & Company, Inc., 1973).
2. E. F. Schumacher, *Small Is Beautiful* (New York: Harper & Row, 1973).
3. Richard Goodwin, *The American Condition* (Garden City, N.Y.: Doubleday & Company, Inc., 1974), p. 328.

CHAPTER 4 *Who Is the Company Run For?*

1. Richard Goodwin, *The American Condition* (Garden City, N.Y.: Doubleday & Company, Inc., 1974), p. 223.
2. *Ibid.*, p. 254.
3. Irving Kristol, "Ethics and the Corporation," *Wall Street Journal*, April 16, 1975.
4. Cf. Richard Armstrong, "The Right Kind of Tax Reform," *Fortune*, December, 1972, p. 86.
5. Cf. Raymond L. Dirks and Leonard Gross, *The Great Wall Street Scandal* (New York: McGraw-Hill Book Company, 1974).

CHAPTER 5 *What Is "Job Philosophy?"*

1. Kurt Mendelssohn, *The Riddle of the Pyramids* (New York: Praeger Publishers, Inc., 1975), p. 153.
2. Kay Withers, *Chicago Tribune*, May 22, 1975.
3. David Pimentel et al., "Energy and Land Constraints in Food Protein Production," *Science*, 190: 754–61, Nov. 21, 1975.

4. Cf. Warren A. Johnson, "The Guaranteed Income as an Environmental Measure," in *Economic Growth vs. the Environment*, Warren A. Johnson and John Hardesty, eds. (Belmont, Calif.: Wadsworth Publishing Co., Inc., 1971).
5. Johnson, *op. cit.,* p. 181.
6. The Nixon administration tried in vain to pass a guaranteed-income bill. (Cf. Daniel P. Moynihan, *The Politics of Guaranteed Income* [New York: Random House, Inc., 1973] and Vincent J. and Vee Burke, *Nixon's Good Deed: Welfare Reform* [New York: Columbia University Press, 1974].)

CHAPTER 6 *Why Do We Work?*

1. Cf. Max Weber, *The Protestant Ethic and the Spirit of Capitalism* (New York: Charles Scribner's Sons, 1948); also, R.H. Tawney, *Religion and the Rise of Capitalism* (New York: Penguin, 1926).
2. Weber, *op. cit.,* pp. 176–7.
3. Richard Wilkinson, *Poverty and Progress* (New York: Praeger Publishers, Inc., 1973), p. 5.
4. Richard Goodwin, *The American Condition* (Garden City, N.Y.: Doubleday & Company, Inc., 1974) pp. 374–5.
5. E. F. Schumacher, "Buddhist Economics," in *Toward a Steady-State Economy*, Herman Daly, ed. (San Francisco: W. H. Freeman and Company Publishers, 1973), p. 232.
6. *Ibid.*
7. Peter Drucker, *The Practice of Management* (New York: Harper & Row, 1954), p. 294.
8. *Ibid.,* p. 298.
9. Douglas McGregor, *The Human Side of Enterprise* (New York: McGraw-Hill Book Company, 1960), pp. 37–8. See also: Abraham Maslow, *The Farther Reaches of Human Nature* (New York: The Viking Press, Inc., 1972).
10. Cf. Walter A. Fairservis, *The Threshold of Civilization* (New York: Charles Scribner's Sons, 1975).
11. Ayn Rand, *Atlas Shrugged* (New York: Random House, Inc., 1957).

Notes

CHAPTER 7 *Can Capitalism Survive?*

1. Garrett Hardin, "The Tragedy of the Commons," *Science*, 162: 1243–8, Dec. 13, 1968.

2. Bruce Hannon, "Energy Conservation and the Consumer," *Science*, 190: 95, Jul. 11, 1975.

3. Cf. S. Fred Singer, ed., *Is There an Optimum Level of Population?* (New York: McGraw-Hill Book Company, 1971).

4. Garrett Hardin in Singer, *op. cit.*, p. 263. Others have made estimates in the same range: cf. Robert S. Mulliken, "Through ZPG to NPG," *Bulletin of the Atomic Scientists*, January, 1974, p. 9, and Joseph J. Spengler in *The 99th Hour, the Population Crisis in the United States*, Daniel O. Price, ed. (Chapel Hill: University of North Carolina Press, 1967), p. 29.

5. Lincoln H. Day, in Singer, *op. cit.*, pp. 277–8.

6. *Population Index*, 34, 4(1968), 471.

7. Day, *loc. cit.*

8. Cf. H.G. Wells, *Men like Gods* (New York: Macmillan, Inc., 1923) and Arthur C. Clarke, *The City and the Stars* (New York: Harcourt Brace Jovanovich, 1956).

9. Jack Parsons, *Population Vs. Liberty* (London: Pemberton Press, 1974).

10. Hardin in Singer, *op. cit.*, p. 262.

11. Cf. Leopold Kohr, *Development Without Aid; The Translucent Society* (Llandy bie, Carmarthenshire, Wales: Christopher Davies [Publisher] Ltd, 1973).

12. Will and Ariel Durant, *The Lessons of History* (New York: Simon & Schuster, Inc., 1968), p. 20.

13. Gerard Piel, *The Acceleration of History* (New York: Alfred A. Knopf, Inc., 1972), p. 369.

14. Kenneth E. Boulding, *The Meaning of the Twentieth Century* (New York: Harper & Row, 1964).

15. J.B.S. Haldane, *The Causes of Evolution* (London: Longmans Green, 1932; paperback reprint, Ithaca, N.Y.: Cornell University Press, 1966). For a recent discussion of the evolutionary basis for group altruism, see: Edward O. Wilson, *Sociobiology* (Cambridge, Mass.: Belknap Press of Harvard University Press, 1975), pp. 106–29.

Notes

16. Hermann J. Muller, in *Man and His Future*, Gordon Wostenholme, ed. (Boston: Little, Brown and Company, 1963), p. 249.
17. William Ophuls, "Leviathan or Oblivion?" in *Toward a Steady-State Economy*, Herman Daly, ed. (San Francisco: W.H. Freeman and Company Publishers, 1973), p. 225.
18. Gurney Breckenfeld, "The Perilous Prospect of a Low-Growth Economy," *Saturday Review*, July 12, 1975.
19. "America's Third Century," *The Economist*, London, October 25, 1975.

CHAPTER 8   *Design for Survival*

1. Marston Bates, *The Forest and the Sea* (New York: Random House, Inc., 1960), p. 261.
2. Roger Revelle, *Science*, 189: 1100, Mar. 21, 1975.
3. Jay Forrester, *Urban Dynamics* (Cambridge, Mass.: The M.I.T. Press, 1969), p. 110.
4. A. V. Hill, "The Ethical Dilemma of Science," *Nature*, 170, 1952, 338–93; also in *Population, Evolution, Birth Control*, Garrett Hardin, ed. (San Francisco: W.H. Freeman and Company Publishers, 1970).
5. Garrett Hardin, *Stalking the Wild Taboo* (Los Altos, Calif.: William Kaufmann, Inc., 1973), p. 181.
6. Freeman J. Dyson, "The Hidden Cost of Saying No," *Bulletin of the Atomic Scientists*, June 1975, p. 23.
7. *Op. cit.*, p. 27.
8. Cf. Will and Ariel Durant, *The Lessons of History* (New York: Simon & Schuster, Inc., 1968), p. 72.
9. Charles Galton Darwin, *The Next Million Years* (Garden City, N.Y.: Doubleday & Company, Inc., 1952), p. 159.
10. Cf., Raymond R. Coffey, *Chicago Daily News*, May 23, 1975.
11. Robert Heilbroner, *An Inquiry into the Human Prospect* (New York: W.W. Norton & Company, Inc., 1974), p. 142.

A Selected Bibliography

Many will question whether growth must really stop. This selection of a few publications from the deluge of opinions, pro and con, includes, I believe, the most important statements on the subject of population, energy, and environmental influences on our human future. Although the balance may be loaded in favor of the need for constraints, opposite views are included.

Alfvén, Hannes and Kerstin. *Living on the Third Planet*. San Francisco: W. H. Freeman and Company, 1972. A Nobel Prize physicist presents a thoughtful synthesis of man's prospects on earth.

Bauer, Raymond A., ed. *Social Indicators*. Cambridge, Mass.: MIT Press, 1966. Can we measure the quality of life? Some practical problems and possible directions.

Beckerman, Wilfred. *Two Cheers for the Affluent Society, A Spirited Defense of Economic Growth*. New York: St. Martin's Press, 1974. ZPG, the author argues, will perpetuate our inequalities; only growth will eliminate poverty.

Berelson, Bernard. "Beyond Family Planning." *Science*, 163: 533–543, Feb. 7, 1969. Reviews twenty-nine different methods of population control beyond family planning.

Borgstrom, Georg. *The Food & People Dilemma*. North Scituate, Mass.: Duxbury Press, 1973. A succinct and authoritative analysis of population pressures on the food supply.

Boulding, Kenneth E. *The Meaning of the Twentieth Century*. New York:

Bibliography

Harper & Row, 1964. A distinguished economist describes the great transition to postcivilization and outlines a strategy for achieving it.

Brown, Harrison. *The Challenge of Man's Future*. New York: The Viking Press, 1954 (paperback). A classic analysis of the food, energy, and population relationships which must determine our future.

————, and Hutchings, Edward, Jr., eds. *Are Our Descendants Doomed?* New York: The Viking Press, 1970 (paperback). A good selection of papers on many aspects of the population problem.

Brown, Lester R. *In the Human Interest, A Strategy to Stabilize World Population*. New York: W. W. Norton & Company, Inc., 1974. Present projections of population increase are found unacceptable. "We may be on the verge of one of the great discontinuities of human history— economic, demographic and political."

————, Patricia L. McGrath and Bruce Stokes, *Twenty-Two Dimensions of the Population Problem, Worldwatch Paper 5,* Washington: Worldwatch Institute, 1976. A summary of the many kinds of impacts of excessive population on our world.

————, with Eckholm, Erik P. *By Bread Alone*. New York: Praeger Publishers, Inc., 1974. An analysis of the food problem, present and future.

Carson, Rachel. *Silent Spring*. Boston: Houghton Mifflin Company, 1962 (paperback). Carson began the environmental revolution with this classic book.

Clark, Wilson. *Energy for Survival, The Alternative to Extinction*. Garden City, N. Y.: Doubleday & Co., Inc., 1974. A thorough and scholarly analysis of our possible sources of energy, concluding that the various kinds of solar energy are our best hope.

Cole, H. S. D.; Freeman, Christopher; Jahoda, Marie; and Pavitt, K.L.R., eds. *Models of Doom, A Critique of The Limits To Growth*. New York: Universe Books, 1973 (paperback). A project team at the University of Sussex (England) attacks the methodology and ideology of Meadows Group, (see below).

Commoner, Barry. *The Closing Circle*. New York: Alfred A. Knopf, Inc., 1972. A leading ecologist blames technology for our environmental problems.

————, *The Poverty of Power,* New York: Alfred A. Knopf, Inc., 1976. Ignorance of the Second Law of Thermo-dynamics leads us to waste irretrievable energy. Excellent analysis, until he begins to draw political conclusions.

Bibliography

• Daly, Herman E., ed. *Toward A Steady-State Economy*. San Francisco: W. H. Freeman and Company, 1973. An excellent collection of readings on how to adjust to a no-growth society.

Darwin, Charles Galton. *The Next Million Years*. Garden City, N. Y.: Doubleday & Co., 1953. The grandson of Charles Darwin forecasts that the population problem will never be solved more than temporarily.

Davis, Kingsley. "Population Policy: Will Current Programs Succeed?" *Science*, 158: 730–39, Nov. 10, 1967. An influential article which argued that, even if people have only the number of children they want, population growth will continue.

Ehrlich, Paul R. and Anne H. *The End of Affluence*. New York: Ballantine Books Inc., 1974 (paperback). The authors of *The Population Bomb* picture our energy-scarce future and how we are getting there.

• Forrester, Jay W. *World Dynamics*. Cambridge, Mass.: Wright-Allen Press, 1971. The precursor to *The Limits To Growth*. Equilibrium must replace growth of our world economy.

Gabor, Dennis. *The Mature Society*. New York: Praeger Publishers Inc., 1971. How do we prevent a successful society from drifting into decadence? This Nobel Prize physicist expresses his opinions clearly and provocatively.

Gray, Elizabeth and David D. and William F. Martin, *Growth and its Implications for the Future*, Branford, Conn.: Dinosaur Press, 1975. An overview of the important work being done and to be done to insure global survival. Asks all the questions.

Hardin, Garrett. *Exploring New Ethics for Survival, The Voyage of the Spaceship Beagle*. New York: The Viking Press, 1972. A fascinating allegory interwoven with a powerful argument, from the leading advocate of population limitation.

————. *Nature and Man's Fate*. New York: Holt, Rinehart and Winston, Inc., 1959. In my opinion, the best and most graphic explanation of how Darwinian evolution actually works. If we are to understand our human problems, we must start here.

Heilbroner, Robert L. *An Inquiry into the Human Prospect*. New York: W. W. Norton & Company, Inc., 1974. An essay on the world predicament of mankind. The challenges of the future will exact a fearful price, but they can be met.

Johnson, Warren A., and Hardesty, John, eds. *Economic Growth vs. the Environment*. Belmont, Calif.: Wadsworth Publishing Co., Inc., 1971. A

Bibliography

careful selection of writings about spaceship earth by economists and ecologists.

Maddox, John. *The Doomsday Syndrome*. New York: McGraw-Hill, Inc. 1972. An attack on the doomsdayers. The author says: "This is not a scholarly work but a complaint."

Malthus, Thomas Robert. *An Essay on the Principle of Population, As it Affects the Future Improvement of Society* (1798). New York: E. P. Dutton & Co., Inc., 1914. While geographical and technological growth kept even with population, Malthus was little regarded. Now we see he was right.

McDonald, Forrest. *The Phaeton Ride*. Garden City, N. Y.: Doubleday & Co., 1974. A cutting blade is applied to our "self-devouring" American society. Abundance for everyone is no longer a possibility for the future.

Meadows, Donella H. and Dennis L.; Randers, Jorgen; and Behrens, William H. III. *The Limits To Growth, a report for the Club of Rome Project on the Predicament of Mankind*. New York: Universe Books, 1972 (paperback). The bombshell which awakened us to the need to plan for our world future. Violently attacked, its basic thesis has survived, scarred but essentially intact.

Mesarovic, Mihajlo, and Pestel, Eduard. *Mankind at the Turning Point, The Second Report to the Club of Rome*. New York: E. P. Dutton & Co., 1974. The sequel to *The Limits To Growth*, modifying but not basically changing its conclusions.

More, Sir Thomas. *Utopia* (1516). Princeton, N. J.: Van Nostrand Reinhold Company, 1947. The originator of the word "utopia" portrayed a heaven-on-earth dull and rigid by our standards.

Nordhaus, William, and Tobin, James. *Is Growth Obsolete?* National Bureau of Economic Research, 50th Anniversary Colloquium V. New York: Columbia University Press, 1972. A scholarly study of the meaning of economic growth.

Paddock, William and Paul, *Famine 1975! America's Decision—Who Will Survive?* Boston: Little, Brown and Co., 1967. Almost a decade ago, they predicted world-wide food shortages. Is triage our solution?

Parsons, Jack. *Population Vs. Liberty*. London, England: Pemberton, 1971; Buffalo, N. Y.: distributed by Prometheus Books (paperback). Excessive population means the practical end of many kinds of freedom. A graphic description of how the quality of life is declining in the United Kingdom.

Pimentel, David; Dritschilo, William; Krummel, John; and Kutzman, John.

Bibliography

"Energy and Land Constraints in Food Protein Production." *Science,* 190: 754–61, Nov. 21, 1975. The pressures of population on food and energy supplies are analyzed.

Ridker, Ronald G., "To Grow or Not to Grow: That's Not the Question," *Science* 182: 1315–18, Dec. 28, 1973. Arguing for unrestrained growth or for no-growth are both cop-outs, he says. Instead, we should attack our economic problems, such as pollution, directly.

Schneider, Stephen H. *The Genesis Strategy, Climate and Global Survival.* New York: Plenum Press, 1976. A "global survival compromise" is one in which the rich nations will have to help the poor to avoid chaos, as the unusually good weather of the last two decades becomes more erratic.

Schumacher, E. F. *Small Is Beautiful, Economics as if People Mattered.* New York: Harper & Row, 1973. Rapidly becoming a classic. A series of essays on our economic problems and how to ease them.

Singer, S. Fred, ed. *Is There an Optimum Level of Population?* New York: McGraw-Hill, Inc. 1971. The outgrowth of a symposium on population size as it relates to quality of life.

Stent, Gunther S. *The Coming of the Golden Age.* Garden City, N. Y.: Natural History Press, 1969. The author argues that, with the inevitable end of progress, a leisurely Golden Age will follow.

Udall, Stewart; Conconi, Charles; and Osterhout, David. *The Energy Balloon.* New York: McGraw-Hill, Inc., 1974. Challenging the vested energy interests, the authors present a program for a lean America.

Vacca, Roberto. *The Coming Dark Age.* Garden City, N. Y.: Doubleday & Co., Inc., 1973. When technology becomes too complex and ties our whole society together in one interdependent network, it faces total collapse.

Watt, Kenneth E. F. *The Titanic Effect, Planning for the Unthinkable.* New York: E. P. Dutton & Co., 1974. Only if we recognize the problems of growth, can we plan how to avoid future crises.

Wilkinson, Richard G. *Poverty and Progress, An Ecological Perspective on Economic Development.* New York: Praeger Publishers, Inc., 1973. An exciting thesis that technological development is primarily a reaction to the pressures of population growth.

Woodward, Herbert N. *The Human Dilemma.* Stamford, Conn.: Brookdale Press, 1971. A Darwinian view of mankind's hopes and prospects.

Young, Louise B., ed. *Population in Perspective.* New York: Oxford University Press, Inc., 1968. Basic readings on population, well edited.

Index

Index

Index

Japan, 16
job philosophy, 95–106, 112–14, 132, 142–43, 175
    definition of, 95–96
Johnson, Warren A., 21 *fn 6*, 22, 23, 123

Kohr, Leopold, 167 *fn 11*
Koughan, Martin, 53
Kristol, Irving, 72–73

labor-intensive activities, 20–24, 118
Latin America, 134–35
legal profession, 98
Legge, John W., 50 *fn 5*
Limits to Growth, The, 4, 5
lumber business, 108–09
Luxembourg, 7

McDonald, Forrest, 39 *fn 2*
McGregor, Douglas, 135–36, 166
McKinsey and Company, 196
malpractice, medical, 191–94
management, British corporate, 196–97
    U. S. corporate, 68–93
management consultants, 43–44
Mankind at the Turning Point, 5
manufacturing burden (overhead), 34–35
marginal-income accounting, 36–37, 39
Massachusetts Institute of Technology (MIT), 4
medical profession, 98
Mendelssohn, Kurt, 101–02
Mississippi (river), 2
More, Thomas, 160
Mostert, Noël, 49 *fn 4*
Moynihan, Daniel P., 123 *fn 6*
Muller, Hermann J., 171

Nature Conservancy, The, 181
Negative Population Growth, 159
net energy, 14, 15
New York Stock Exchange, 79, 105
no-growth (steady-state) economy, 1, 25, 116, 159, 164, 177

noise, level of, 48
North Sea, 162
Northrop Aviation Corporation, 90–91
nuclear power, 12–13, 151

Odum, Howard T., 11
oil, 7, 8–11, 12
oil tankers, 48–49
Ophuls, William, 172
Organization of Petroleum Exporting Countries (OPEC), 10–11
overhead (manufacturing burden), 34–35
ozone layer, 139–40

Parsons, Jack, 162
Piel, Gerard, 170–71
Pimentel, David, 120 *fn 3*
Plato, 160, 169
Polaroid Corporation, 73
pollution, 17, 18
population, ability to sustain, 152–53
    basic problem, the, 154–55
    optimum level of, 155–63
    relation to energy and environment, 2–4
    replacement birth rate, 5, 6
    U. S. census figures, 5–7
Population Bomb, The, 4
predestinarianism, 126–27
price mechanism, 13, 15, 17
primogeniture, 158
productivity, 19–20
public works, 120–22
pyramids, Egyptian, construction of, 101–02, 109–10

Rand, Ayn, 138
refrigerators, distribution of, 61–63
responsibility, individual, 179–195
Revelle, Roger, 183
Russia, 16

Saab, 132–133
Sahara Desert, 16
Sahel, African, famines in, 8

215

Index

This book was produced for the publisher by
Ray Freiman & Company, Stamford, Connecticut.